Popular Milk Glass
& Other Opaque Novelties

Douglas Congdon-Martin

Schiffer Publishing Ltd®
4880 Lower Valley Road, Atglen, PA 19310 USA

A Note About Values

The values given in this volume are gathered from dealers, collectors and auctions and are for items in good condition with no chips, cracks or flakes. The selling prices are always changing and the values in this volume should not be used in buying or selling. They are only a guide. The publisher and author are not responsible for any loss if not used as intended

Library of Congress Cataloging-in-Publication Data

Congdon-Martin, Douglas.
Popular milk glass & other opaque novelties / by Douglas Congdon-Martin.
p. cm.
ISBN 0-7643-2207-9 (pbk.)
1. Milk glass—United States—History. I. Title: Popular milk glass and other opaque novelties. II. Title.

NK5439.M54C66 2005
748.2—dc22

2004026854

Designed by Mark David Bowyer
Type set in Embassy BT / Zurich BT

ISBN: 0-7643-2207-9
Printed in China
1 2 3 4

Published by Schiffer Publishing Ltd.
4880 Lower Valley Road
Atglen, PA 19310
Phone: (610) 593-1777; Fax: (610) 593-2002
E-mail: Info@schifferbooks.com

For the largest selection of fine reference books on this and related subjects, please visit our web site at
www.schifferbooks.com
We are always looking for people to write books on new and related subjects. If you have an idea for a book please contact us at the above address.

This book may be purchased from the publisher.
Include $3.95 for shipping.
Please try your bookstore first.
You may write for a free catalog.

In Europe, Schiffer books are distributed by
Bushwood Books
6 Marksbury Ave.
Kew Gardens
Surrey TW9 4JF England
Phone: 44 (0) 20 8392-8585; Fax: 44 (0) 20 8392-9876
E-mail: info@bushwoodbooks.co.uk
Free postage in the U.K., Europe; air mail at cost.

Contents

Acknowledgments 4
Introduction 5
Akro-Agate 6
Atterbury Glass Co. 8
Avon 18
Belmont Glass Company 20
Boston & Sandwich Glass Company 21
Boyd Crystal Art Glass 22
Challinor, Taylor & Co. 24
Consolidated 29
Cooperative Flint Glass Co., Ltd. 30
Degenhart: Crystal Art Glass Company 32
John A. Dobson & Company 35
Eagle Glass & Manufacturing Company 36
Fenton Art Glass Company 37
E.C. Flaccus Company 40
Gillinder 44
H. Greener & Co. 45
Greentown: Indiana Tumbler & Goblet Co. 46
K. R. Haley Glassware Company 49
Hazel Atlas Glass Company 50
Imperial Glass Co. 52
Indiana Glass Co. 57
Jeannette Glass Company 58
Kanawha Glass Company 59
Kemple Glass Company 60
MacBeth-Evans Glass Company 63
McKee & Bros. 64
Mosser Glass Company 72
Rosso Wholesale Glass Dealers, Inc. 73
David Schepps 74
L.E. Smith 75
Summit Art Glass 77
Vallerystahl • Portieux • PV France 78
Westmoreland Specialty Company (WSC)
• Westmoreland Glass Company 94
L.G. Wright 117
R. & G.A. Wright 123
Miscellaneous Milk Glass 124
- Covered Dishes & Bowls 124
- Jars 133
- Open Dishes and Bowls 135
- Compotes 137
- Plates 138
- Drinking Vessels 146
- Pitchers, Creamers & Sugars, & Carafes . 148
- Decanters & Flasks 150
- Shakers 151
- Open Salts 152
- Egg Cups 152
- Toothpicks 153
- Vanity and Toilet Wares 154
- Smoking Accessories & Matchholders ... 156
- Vases & Wall Pockets 156
- Lighting 158
- Figural Glass 158
- Easter Eggs 159

Bibliography 160

Acknowledgments

My sincerest thanks goes to the kind folks at Aumann Auction Center in Nokomis, Illinois. Kurt Aumann and Dan Matthews were kind enough to tell me about the upcoming auction of the great Lucy Tarbox collection and invite me out to take pictures. To make it work they set up the auction early and let me invade their auction house to do the photography for this book. The whole team in Nokomis was gracious and kind, and I thank them for their work. They have ongoing auctions covering a broad range of collectibles and antiques. You can call them toll free at 1-888-282-8648 (888-auctn-4u) or visit their informative website at aumannauctions.com.

I also owe a great deal of thanks to Bob Sanford. I was privileged to work with him on his last book *Victorian Glass Novelties,* as photographer and editor, and am looking forward to his next. Bob kindly shared his expertise regarding current prices and provided me with a wealth of information about company histories.

As always, producing a book is a team effort, and I thank all of the folks here at Schiffer Publishing that lent their talents and creativity to this process.

Introduction

The collector's fascination with milk glass and other opaque glass can be linked to many factors. The greatest of these is its innate beauty. At its best, milk glass is sculptural. Like good sculpture its faceted surfaces give play to the light, so that, depending on where you stand or the time of day, the glass will take on different and captivating looks. While many of the moulds used for milk glass also gave birth to more transparent forms of glass, the milk glass examples have a solidity that brings up their design, letting us clearly see the creativity and craft of the mould maker.

Another factor is its history. As you will see in the brief descriptions of the companies that produced milk glass, its history in America covers a century and a half. Glassmaking was part of the industrial strength of our nation and in some parts of it, western Pennsylvania, Ohio, and West Virginia, it was an essential element in the economy, contributing to the well-being of thousands of workers. It is interesting to see the movement of people, equipment, and even moulds as the industry evolved over 150 years.

The third factor is the variety of forms milk glass has taken. From plates to planters, covered dishes to perfume bottles, the plasticity of glass has allowed mould makers to include high levels of detail and complexity in their work. And that work ranges from the artistic to the mundane, from the perfect gift to the most necessary of implements. And all of it, for the true collector, is beautiful and desirable.

Finally, milk glass is available. It was and is made in massive amounts, and even though it is glass and much has fallen victim to the human fumbles, much survives. There are rarities of course, many of them appearing in this book and many more covered in *The Milk Glass Book* by Frank Chiarenza and James Slater (Schiffer Publishing, 1998). Prices for these can range into the thousands of dollars and most collectors would love to find them at any price. But there are also more common items that are still beautiful and desirable, and have the added advantage of being affordable. This makes the hobby fun and open to new collectors as well as old. It is an area of collecting where you can begin small and work your way up as your interest and your pocketbook grows.

The National Milk Glass Collectors Society (NMGCS)

Thousands of collectors have discovered milk glass already and they are ready to share their enthusiasm with the neophyte. The National Milk Glass Collectors Society has been official since 1987, though they trace their roots even earlier. They have held annual conventions since 1983 as places to share their knowledge and love of milk glass, make new friends, and place to sell and buy milk glass from other enthusiasts. The NMGCS website is full of useful information about milk glass and the Society's meetings and activities. It is found at nmgcs.org. Visit them today.

Akro-Agate

Akron, Ohio • Clarksburg, West Virginia

c.1910–1951

Akro Agate started life as a marble manufacturer in Akron, Ohio. Working from a room over the Wagner Marsh Shoe Store, Dr. George T. Rankin and Gilbert C. Marsh built their own machinery and produced various sized "glassies" which they sold in packages of 25 for fifty cents. Their trademark, "Akro Agate" was applied for in March, 1911 and approved in August, 1911.

Along with Horace C. Hill, Rankin and Marsh formed the Akro Agate Company, and met with enough success that in late 1914 they moved to a larger building in Clarksburg, West Virginia.

The company's success continued in Clarksburg, owing in large part to technological innovations and automation. Their production methods allowed them to produce high quality marbles in numbers great enough to permit an affordable price.

The edge they had gained from technology was somewhat eroded in the early 1930s by successful patent challenges. Seeking ways to strengthen the business in the face of renewed competition, they began to broaden their line to include ashtrays, glass containers, and children's plates. Included among the glass containers were figural powder jars in many forms, of which the most popular were a Scotty Dog and a Colonial Lady.

After experiencing strong sales during the Second World War, sales dropped in the aftermath and by 1949 production had ceased, though they continued to sell items from stock until 1951.

The facts in this brief description were gleaned from a wonderful book by Roger and Claudia Hardy, *The Complete Line of the Akro Agate Co.* To learn more about the company, including some photographs, or to order the Hardy's book, visit: mkl.com/akro/club on the web.

Akro Agate milk glass Lady with Fan covered dish. $48.

Akro Agate milk glass Scotty Dog covered dishes. Left, light pink; right: white. $55;$45.

Akro Agate(?) Rabbit covered dish, it is made of a very deep olive colored glass, top is not marked, bottom has Akro Agate mark, the two pieces seem to match up. $70.

Rare purple color Atterbury Hen on Basket Base, 7 inches. $875.

Atterbury Glass Co.

Pittsburgh, Pennsylvania

1860–1903?

Atterbury Glass began in Pittsburgh as Hale, Atterbury & Co. in 1860, the partnership of James and Thomas Atterbury and their brother-in-law James Hale, who became the firm's first glassblower. Their White House Factory was located at Carson and McKee streets in Pittsburgh's South Side. When Hale left the firm after two years, he was replaced by James Reddick, who was to leave Atterbury in 1864. These changes in the ownership configuration led to a series of name changes, from Hale, Atterbury & Co. to Atterbury, Reddick & Co. to Atterbury & Co., and finally to the Atterbury Glass Co. in 1893.

Atterbury produced a wide range of products including tableware, bar bottles, and lamps. Among the leaders in the production of glass lamps, Atterbury exhibited at the 1876 Centennial Exhibition in Philadelphia where it was given an award for its designs. Of lamp chimneys and globes.

To milk glass collectors it is best known for its covered dishes in the forms of rabbits, ducks, chicks, and bull's, and boar's heads. These dishes made their appearance in the 1880s with patents dating to 1886 for the "Rabbit," c. 1887 for the "Duck," and around 1888 for the "Boar's Head." Other dishes followed, including "Chick and Eggs," "Hen on Nest," "Reclining Cat," "Swan," "Reclining Lion," "Entwined Fish," "Reclining Fox," and "Hand Holding a Bird

While there is some confusion about it demise, Atterbury appears to have remained an independent factory until 1903.

Two useful websites provided the facts about Atterbury and have much more information for the interested collector. They are: carnegielibrary.org and gransplace.com.

Atterbury (?) milk glass Retriever Tray. $85.

Atterbury Cat on Lacy Base, green glass eyes, dated 1889. $400.

Atterbury 7-inch Hen on Basket. $110.

Atterbury 7-inch Hen on Basket. $110.

Atterbury blue milk glass 7-inch Hen on Basket Base. $150.

Atterbury blue milk glass 7-inch Hen on Basket Base. $135.

Atterbury Hen on Lacy Base with blue marble top, glass eyes both different. $400.

Atterbury Hen on Lacy Base with cased blue glass head. $225.

Atterbury milk glass 7-inch Hen on Basket Base with blue milk glass head. $210.

Atterbury milk glass 7-inch Hen on Basket Base with blue cased glass head. $160.

Atterbury milk glass Hen on Basket Base with pale green marbling, green glass eyes. $135.

Atterbury, 7-inch Hen on Basket covered dish. $110.

Atterbury Chick on Pile of Eggs on lacy base with glass eyes, dated 1889. $140.

Atterbury milk glass tall Owl jar. $110.

Atterbury Hand and Dove covered dish, top dated 1889, lacy base. $110.

Atterbury, 7 inches Hand and Dove on Lacy Base covered dish.

Atterbury full body Duck. $175.

Atterbury Raised-Wing Swan on Lacy Base covered dish. $185.

Atterbury milk glass Bird & Wheat mug. $38.

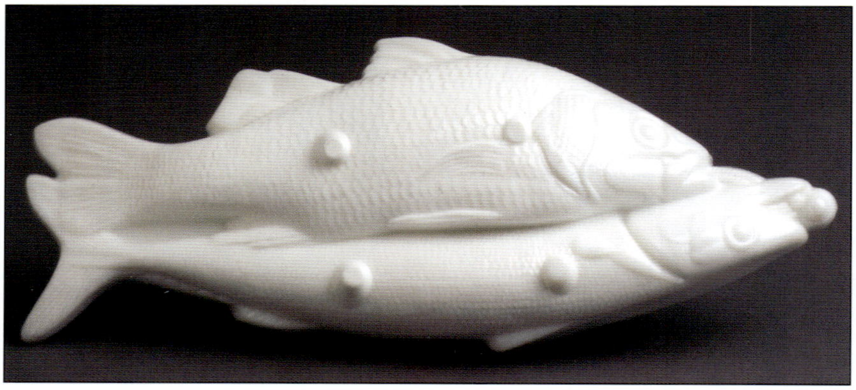

Atterbury Double Fish pickle. $150.

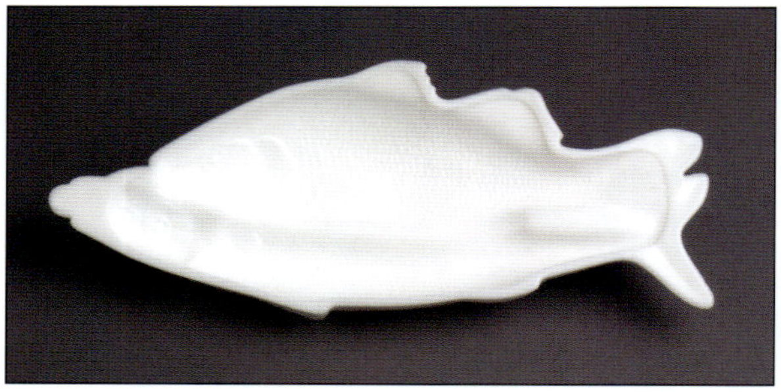

Atterbury Fish plate. $55.

Atterbury Entwined Fish covered dish with red eyes, open lace rim; top dated 1889. $185.

Atterbury milk glass Walking Fish covered dish with glass eyes. $500+

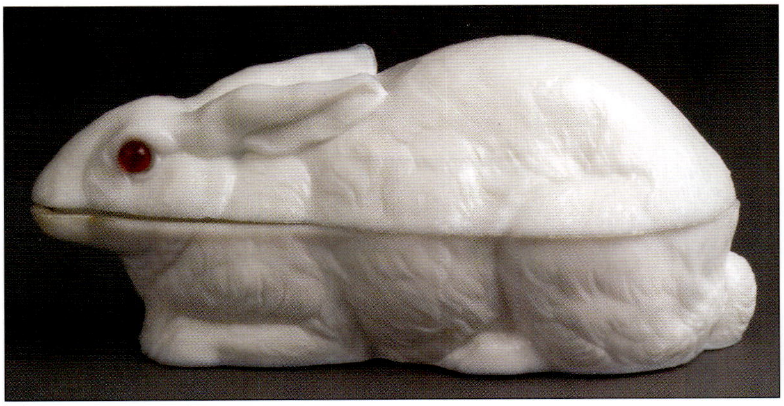

Atterbury full body Rabbit covered dish, 7 inches. $150.

Atterbury Boar's Head covered dish, dated 1889. $750.

Atterbury Lion on Lacy Base covered dish, dated 1889. $145.

Atterbury Bull's Head mustard. $125.

Atterbury Bull's Head mustards. Left: blue, has no ladle; right: opalescent, has ladle. $125; $75.

Atterbury milk glass Fox on Ribbed Base covered dish with no eyes, dated 1889. $130.

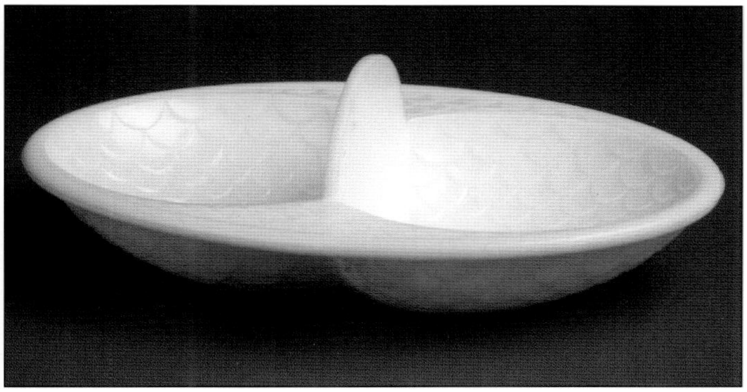

Atterbury divided dish. $42.

Atterbury (?) milk glass Sugar Melon with Leaf covered dish. $85.

Avon

Suffern, New York • New York, New York

1886–Present

Avon Products, an international merchandiser of beauty and home products, began as an outgrowth of David McConnell's door-to-door book sales business. After finding a demand for good perfumes, McConnell and his wife developed some fragrances and began to sell them along with the books. Before long the book sales were dwarfed by the demand for perfume, and in 1886 the California Perfume Company was born in Suffern, New York. In 1928 a line of products was introduced called Avon, and in 1939 Avon Products became the official name of the company.

Avon has never manufactured glass, but has used glass items as containers for its cosmetic and personal care products. According to Mark Pickvet, glass items were introduced as early as the 1920s. It has also commissioned others to make glass products for them. In the 1960s Wheaton Glass in New Jersey created a line of decorative containers for them. Wheaton also produced a line of glass dinnerware for Avon, the 1876 Cape Cod Collection, which was produced from 1975 to 1993. Nearly all of the Avon milk glass was originally produced as containers.

Little is written about Avon glass. Debbie and Randy Coe's book, *Avon's 1876 Cape Cod Collection,* has some information on the company, as does Pickvet's *Encyclopedia of Glass*. Both are published by Schiffer Books and were referenced for this essay.

Avon blue Love Birds on Base. $28.

Avon blue milk glass Cuckoo Bird fragrance bottle. $28.

Avon white Bird covered bowl. $28.

Avon White Hen on Brown Base. $28.

Avon milk glass Owl fragrance bottle. $28.

Avon milk glass Lamb fragrance bottle. $28.

Avon milk glass Golf Ball fragrance bottle. $28.

Belmont Glass Company

Bellaire, Ohio

1865–1890

The Belmont Glass Company was organized in March, 1865, by John Robinson, Charles Henry Over, Henry Faupel, and W.G. Barnard under the name of Barnes, Faupel & Co., and was not incorporated until two years later, when it became the Belmont Glass Company. They began by producing crystal glass tableware and added color in 1885. Failing to make a go of it they liquidated their moulds (to Crystal Glass Company and Central Glass Company) in 1890. The building was razed in 1893.

Information about Belmont is scarce. What we have found came primarily from Mark Pickvet's *Encyclopedia of Glass,* a great resource for collectors. It is published by Schiffer Books.

Belmont Glass milk glass Monkey by Hat toothpick, 3 x 3.5 inches. $90.

Boston & Sandwich Glass Company

Sandwich, Massachusetts

1825-c.1888

Boston & Sandwich Glass Company began as Sandwich Manufacturing Company in 1825, changing its name in 1826. Under the leadership of its founder, Deming Jarves, it first produced blown glass, but became known for it pressed glass. During the middle of the nineteenth century, Boston & Sandwich was one of the most successful glass houses in the United States. A labor strike in 1887, caused the company to close its doors, though a group of employees continued to produced a small amount of glass under the name Sandwich Cooperative Glass Company. There venture did not last long.

For more information see Pickvet's *Encyclopedia of Glass* and Kaiser and Barlow's expansive series: *Sandwich Glass*, both published by Schiffer. Information was drawn from these excellent sources for this brief essay.

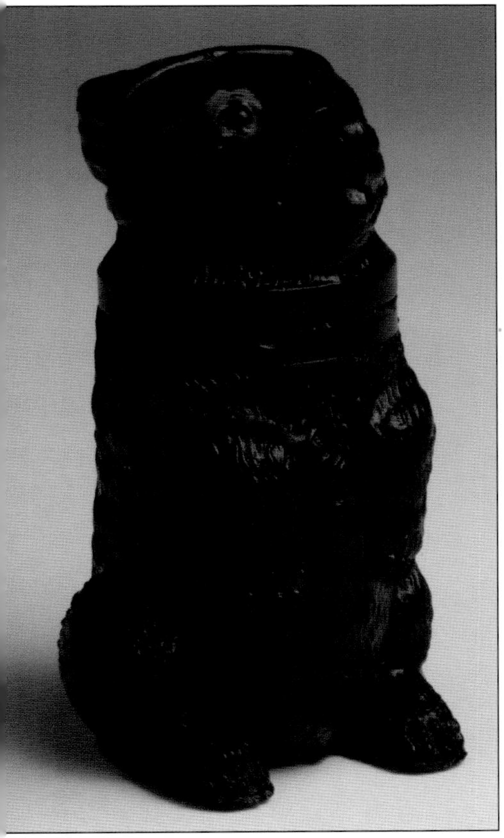

Sandwich black glass Bear Jar, 3.75 inches tall. $350.

Sandwich Glass opaque milk glass Spaniel Dog covered dish, diamond and stippled base. $800.

Boyd Crystal Art Glass

Cambridge, Ohio

1978–Present

The father and son team of Bernard C. and Bernard F. Boyd opened Boyd's Crystal Glass in Cambridge, Ohio, on October 10, 1978. Bernard C., the father, had spent many years in the glass business, starting at age 16 at Cambridge Glass, where his father, Zack Boyd, also worked. He was employed by Degenhart Glass in 1978, when the owner, Elizabeth Degenhart, died. In her will she stipulated that Boyd should have the first option to purchase the business, which he did, along with all but 15 of the moulds, which were retired. The senior Boyd died on August 5, 1988, after a brief illness, but the business continued with his son and his grandson, John B. Boyd. The family tradition and its formulas and secrets have continued to produce hand-moulded, high quality glass into the fourth generation.

For more information including historic photos and company marks visit boydglass.com and glassencyclopedia.com.

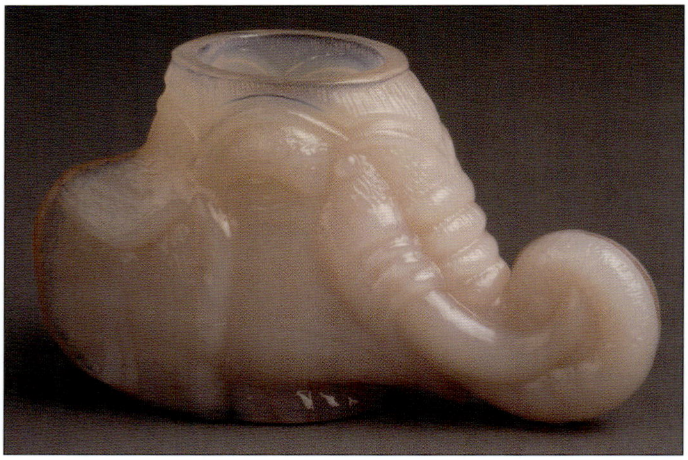

Boyd Elephant Head toothpick. $10.

Boyd Bird with Berry on Base. $28.

Boyd chocolate Lamb on Basket. $28.

Three Boyd Hen on Base covered dishes, green milk glass, beige milk glass, and pink milk glass, 5.5 inches. $28.

Two Boyd Hobo Shoes. $35 each.

Challinor, Taylor & Co.

Tarentum, Pennsylvania

1885–1891, succeeded by U.S. Glass Co.

In 1885 Challinor, Taylor & Co. was organized by David Challinor, David Taylor, and James Challinor. The firm was well known for its tableware, novelties, opal ware, opaque and mosaic glass ware. David Challinor held the patent for mosaic (marble) glass. In 1891 the firm became a part of the United States Glass Co. as Factory "C". Some of their tableware patterns include Blockade, Oval Panel, Hobnail with Bars, Double Fan, Flower & Panel, Opaque Scroll and Tree of Life.

The information is shared courtesy of Bob Sanford, author of *Victorian Glass Novelties,* published by Schiffer Books.

Challinor, Taylor 5-inch Hen on Bulging Rim Base, black glass. $120 each.

Challinor, Taylor clear Rooster on Basket Base with original painted top and comb. $280.

Challinor, Taylor Dominecker Hen on Basket Base covered dishes, 7 inches. Left: has very nice paint; right: very nice paint. $250; $150.

Two Challinor, Taylor 5-inch Hen on Bulging Rim Base, one is milk glass with blue milk glass head, one is black glass. $120 each.

Challinor, Taylor milk glass Rooster on Basket Base with painted comb, 7 inches. $130.

Challinor, Taylor milk glass Rooster on Basket Base, 7 inches. $130.

Challinor, Taylor aqua & butterscotch Flying Swan covered sugar, missing the lid. $65.

Challinor, Taylor milk glass large & small Owl Pitchers. Large: $85; small: $60.

Challinor, Taylor Block Swan covered dish, it is the 6.25 x 8 inches version. $185.

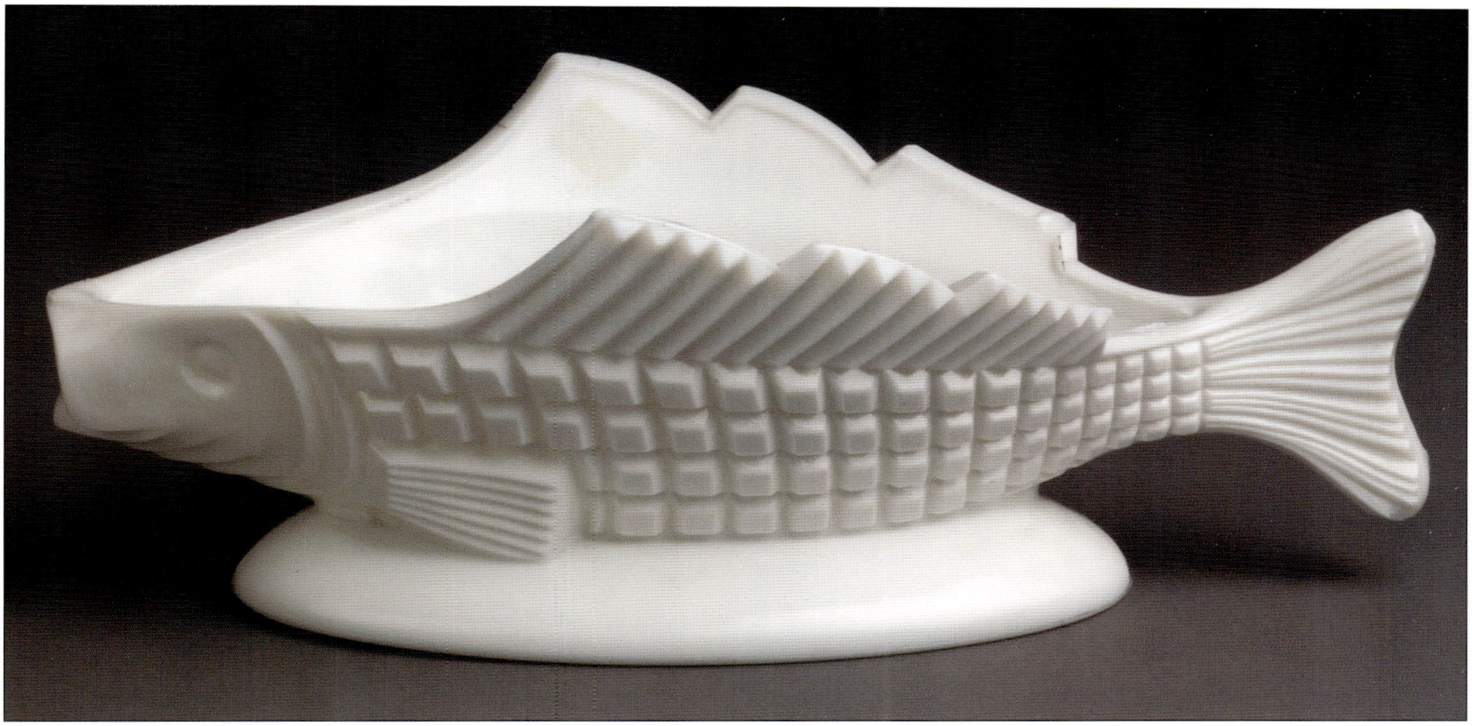

Challinor, Taylor milk glass Waffle Fish pickle dish. $200.

Two blue Owl creamers, Challinor, Taylor Co. $45 each

Challinor, Taylor blue milk glass Tree of Life syrup. $145.

Green cruet, Challinor, Taylor Co., Forget-Me-Not pattern. $145.

Green shaker, Challinor, Taylor Co., Forget-Me-Not pattern. $85.

Round Challinor, Taylor plate with pierced peg rim. $42.

Six Challinor, Taylor blue milk glass Scroll tumblers. $55 each.

Consolidated

Coraopolis, Pennsylvania

1893-1964

Consolidated Lamp & Glass Company was founded in the merger of the Wallace and McAfee Company and Fostoria Shade and Lamp. After a fire at the plant in Fostoria, Ohio, they built a new facility in Coraopolis, Pennsylvania in 1895.

Concentrating primarily on lamps, globes, and shades, they also developed a line of milk glass. The company was sold to Dietz Brothers in 1962 and closed in 1964 following a fire that destroyed most of the factory.

Consolidated Glass Pitcher with gold flecks. $85.

Cooperative Flint Glass Co., Ltd. (Flint Coop)

Beaver Falls, Pennsylvania

1879–?

The Cooperative Flint Glass Co. was organized in 1879 at Beaver Falls, Pennsylvania. The men involved included William and Phillip Scharff, E. T. Dunn, Joseph Brown, and Charles W Klein. In 1888 Charles W. Klein and E. T. Dunn resigned and traveled to Findlay, Ohio, to help organize the Findlay Flint Glass Co. A fire caused extensive damage in 1889 and the plant was rebuilt. Charles W. Klein evidently returned after the Findlay Flint factory burned in 1891 and was not rebuilt. This factory produced novelties, lamps, bridge sets, lunch sets, dinner sets, beer mugs, furniture knobs, stamp plates, sundries, tumblers, paperweights, inks, sponge cups, and pattern tableware. Their tableware patterns include Columbia, Daisy, Mandolin, Royal, Forest, Imperial, Colonial, Unique, Magna, Famous, 20th Century, Regina, Lily, Douglas, Ray, #130 Currier & Ives, Rex, Radiant, Art Navo, La France, Martha Washington and Swan. Their novelties and sundries include the Frog toothpick, Anvil salt and ornate Flytraps.

Flint Coop milk glass Walking Bear unsigned. $2500.

Flint Coop? camphor Glass Elephant covered dish unsigned. $85.

Flint Coop? milk glass Elephant bottom and black top unsigned. $110.

Degenhart: Crystal Art Glass Company

Cambridge, Ohio

1947–1978

The Crystal Art Glass Company of Cambridge, Ohio, was started by John and Elizabeth Degenhart in 1947. Both had had long experience in the glass industry. John's father, Andrew, had been a mouldmaker for several glass companies in the Midwest, including Hobbs, Brockunier in Dunkirk, Indiana, and the Dalzell Glass Company in Findlay Ohio. John became the foreman of press shop at Cambridge Glass where he retired after many years of service. Elizabeth also worked at Cambridge Glass for a time, beginning when she was 16 years old and continuing until she married John in 1908, when she left to take up house keeping and, later, ran an antique business.

At home John engaged in the art of making paperweights, for which he became quite renowned. Some of these were designed or decorated by Elizabeth. After John's retirement, the stage was set, in 1947, for the establishment of Crystal Art Glass, at 1203 Morton Avenue in Cambridge, a small cinder block building. There a small staff consisting of John, the glassmaker, John Wilson, an assistant, and Elizabeth, the bookkeeper and sales manager produced a line of glassware, paperweights, and novelty glass.

When John died in May, 1964, Elizabeth continued the business, maintaining the product line and adding new modern designs to it. Upon her death she stipulated that Bernard C. Boyd, her glassmaker, should have first option on the business. He acted on the opportunity and he and his son, Bernard F., began Boyd Glass, continuing the tradition to the present day.

For more information visit the Degenhart Museum website at degenhartmuseum.com. Many of the facts in this brief description were gathered there.

Degenhart blue and custard milk glass Bird with Berry on Base covered dishes. $38 each.

Degenhart custard Bird with Berry on Split Rib Base. $35.

Degenhart green Bird with Berry. $35.

Degenhart white Bird with Berry. $35.

Degenhart pink Turkey. $35.

Degenhart light custard Turkey on Split Rib Base. $38.

Degenhart gray slag Turkey on Base. $35.

Degenhart Lamb on Base. $35.

Degenhart pink and green opaque Lamb on Split Rib Base covered dishes. $35 each.

Elizabeth Degenhart plate, fading paint. $50.

Elizabeth Degenhart, "First Lady of Glass," Angel Head plate with pierced rim, painted. $50.

John A. Dobson & Company

Baltimore, Maryland

c. 1900

Robed Santa on Sleigh, Dobson & Co. The design was patented May 21, 1901 by Harry T. Thomas (Design No 34,527). He assigned his patent to John A, Dobson and Company of Baltimore, Maryland. $110.

Eagle's Head Sleigh salt, Dobson & Co. Very rare. $110.

Eagle Glass & Manufacturing Company

Wellsburg, West Virginia

1895–1917

The Eagle Glass & Manufacturing Company of Wellsburg (Lazearville), West Virginia was organized in 1895 by James, Joseph, H. W. and Samuel Paull, all brothers. After a fire in 1902 and a reorganization in 1911, they stopped producing glassware in 1917 when they turned their efforts to metal ware. Most of their glassware production was in opal and milk glass and the items included novelties, toothpick holders, salt shakers, vanity sets , lamps, syrups and sugar shakers.

Thanks to Bob Sanford for this information.

Eagle Glass bon bon dish. $38.

Eagle Glass Co.? Lion on scroll base covered dish. $85.

Eagle Glass Co.? American Hen on scroll base covered dish. $50.

Fenton Art Glass Company

Williamstown, West Virginia

1905–Present

From the company history:

"The Fenton Art Glass Company was founded in 1905 by Frank L. Fenton and his brother John W. Fenton in an old glass factory building in Martins Ferry, Ohio. They began by painting decorations on glass blanks made by other glass manufacturers. Soon, being unable to get the glass they needed, they decided to produce their own glass. The first glass from the new Fenton factory in Williamstown, West Virginia, was made on January 2, 1907.

"Frank L. Fenton's desire to develop new and unusual colors helped to keep Fenton in the forefront of the handmade art glass industry. During the years from 1905 to the 1920s, Fenton design was heavily influenced by the artists at Tiffany and Steuben...

"During the 1930's and 1940's, Fenton produced practical items, such as mixing bowls and tableware to get through the depression and WWII shortages. They continued working on developing a wide array of new colors.

"In the late 1940's, the top three members of the Fenton management team died, leaving Frank M. Fenton, age 33, and Wilmer C. (Bill) Fenton, age 25, to step in and take over as President and Vice President. In spite of other glass factories closing at a rapid rate, Frank and Bill led the Fenton factory through significant American growth for the next 30 years.

"In 1986, the leadership of the company passed on to the third generation, with George W. Fenton, Frank M.'s son, taking over as President."

For historical photos and more information about Fenton Art Glass visit the company website at fentonartglass.com. Also be sure to see John Walk's *The Big Book of Fenton Milk Glass: 1940-1985* (Schiffer Books).

Fenton blue milk glass Hen with Eggs on Base covered dishes, 5.5 inches. $38.

Fenton Eagle bicentennial paper weight. $28.

Fenton light blue slag glass Hen with Eggs on Base covered dish, 5.5 inches. $35.

Fenton milk glass Hen with Eggs on Base covered dish, 5.5 inches. $35.

Fenton slag glass and amethyst with a milk glass head Hen with Eggs on Base covered dishes, 5.5 inches. $35.

Fenton painted Hen on Base. $42.

Fenton Hobnail Shoe covered dish. $28.

Fenton Silver Crest Fan vase with painted violets. $20.

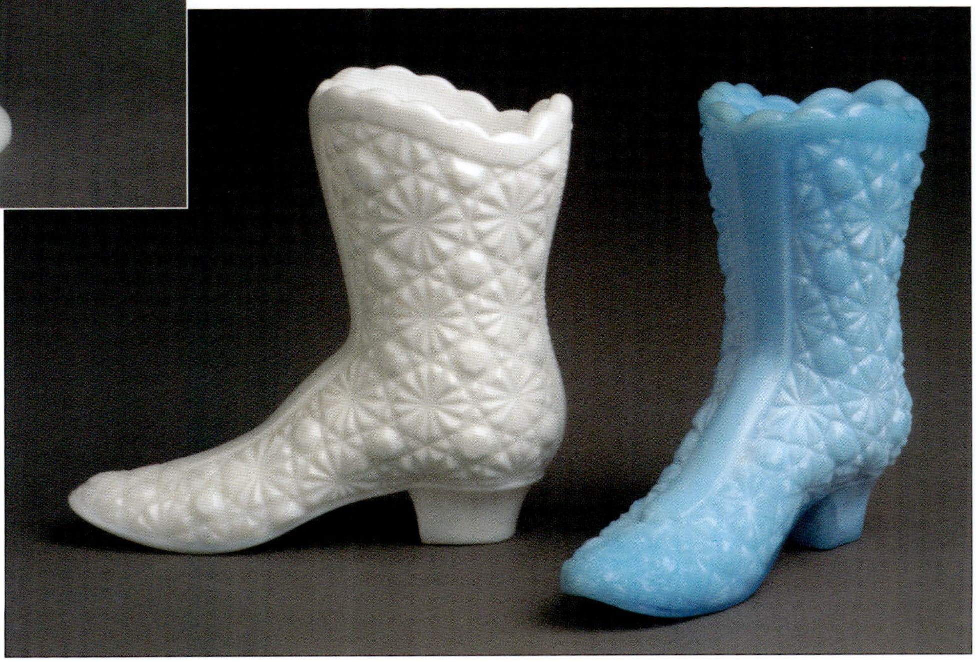

Two Fenton Hightop Shoes, Daisy and Button. $10 each.

E.C. Flaccus Company

Wheeling, West Virginia

1877–1906

Flaccus began in Wheeling, West Virginia, in 1877 as G.C. Flaccus & Son, a food packagers and distributors. G.C. was George C., the father, and the son was George A. In 1879 the name was changed to Flaccus Bros., and after the father retired, three brothers, George A., William C., and Edward C., were the owners. In 1885 William left the company and his son, Charles C. joined. Around 1898 Edward C. left the firm to form his own company, E.C. Flaccus Co.

Though its name is on the glass, E.C. Flaccus was not a glass company. Instead they bought their containers from other companies, including, perhaps, the C.L. Flaccus Company of Tarentum, Pennsylvania.

Other manufacturers mentioned as possible suppliers of animal covered dishes are Frank Glass, Eagle Glass, or Ball & Crowl of Wellsburg, West Virginia, or Central Glass of Wheeling. Dishes seem to have been concentrated in the years 1898-1900.

A wealth of information about Flaccus and other glass companies can be found at gransplace.com, to which we are indebted for the facts presented here.

Flaccus Dove covered dish. $135.

Flaccus Hen on Chick Base. $140.

Flaccus Hen on Chick Base. $140.

Flaccus Fish on Skiff covered dish. $135.

Flaccus Dolphin on Sauce Boat. $95.

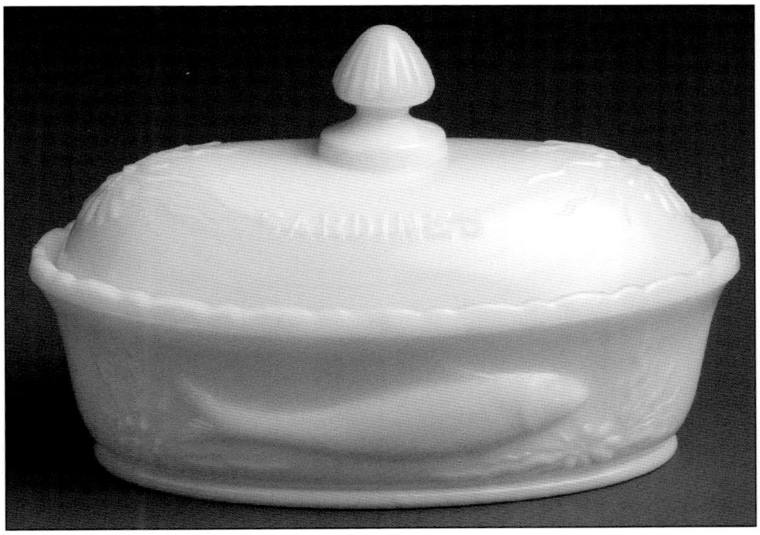

Flaccus Sardines covered dish. $60.

Flaccus Crawfish on Scroll Base, some paint remaining on rim. $120.

Flaccus Deer on Fallen Tree Base. $275.

Flaccus Dog on Wheat Base. $300.

Flaccus Jack Rabbit. $120.

Flaccus Turtle on Scroll Base. $125.

Flaccus Wooly Lamb on Bo Peep Base. $150.

Flaccus Dewey on Tile Base. $85.

Flaccus Battleship Wheeling. $45.

Flaccus Uncle Sam on Battle Ship. $45.

Gillinder

Philadelphia, Pennsylvania •
Port Jervis, New York, 1861–Present

Gillinder is one of America's oldest glass companies. Its roots go back to the William T. Gillinder, who began working in the glass factories of the English Midlands as a boy of 8. A talented young man, he mastered the rudiments of glass chemistry by age 16 and was teaching adults about the art of making glass.

While he was experiencing success, the glass industry in England experienced a decline, so, with his wife and four children, he set off for America, and after a rocky start, founded the Flint Glass Works in Philadelphia in 1861. His sons, James and Frederic joined the company in 1867, when it was renamed Gillinder & Sons.

At the 1876 Centennial Exhibition in Philadelphia, the company set up an actual glassmaking operation. They delighted the crowds and by some accounts sold over 100,000 glass "Cinderella" slippers, in addition to other souvenirs.

At about this same time, Gillinder produced milk glass eggs for the easter season. Often painted and sometimes embossed, these eggs were popular gifts from a gentleman to a woman in his life, according to Debbie Coe.

The business stayed in the family and, in 1912, three of his grandsons, moved the business to Port Jervis, New York, having acquired a vacant glass factory. They renamed the company Gillinder Brothers, Inc., and it continues at the same factory, operated by the sixth generation of Gillinders. The business today is very successful in the fields of commercial and industrial glass, producing among other things nearly 50% of the runway lights used in U.S. airports. But they also continue producing glass giftware items, as they have for well over 100 years, often using the vintage moulds from their archives.

For further information on Gillinder glass visit their company website at gillinderglass.com and be sure to read the interesting article by Debbie Coe at kaleden.com/articles/3148.

Swan Master salt, no Chariot, Gillinder & Sons. $125-150.

H. Greener & Co.

Sunderland, England

1858–?

Henry Greener and James Angus formed the Wear Flint Glass Works in 1858 at Sunderland, England. When Angus died in 1869 Greener took possession of the company and led it through a period of growth in the 1870s under the name of Greener Glass. They were known for fancy wares and commemorative pieces.

In 1882 Henry Greener died and business was taken over by his son, Edwin. In 1885 the company was renamed H. Greener & Co. and was issued a new trademark, but it faced rising debt and, in 1886, was sold to its principal financier, James Augustus Jobling. In 1921 the company was renamed James A. Jobling and Company, became the first in England to produce PYREX in Great Britain, and developed a line of high quality pressed glass. It eventually became a part of Corning Glass and continues in operation today.

Further information can be found at: glassencyclopedia.com and at: murrayam @supanet.com, the sources for these facts about Greener Glass.

H. Greener & Co. purple slag glass Reclining Cow covered dish. *Glass Collector's Digest* says it is from the 1878 and is rare. $1100.

Greentown: Indiana Tumbler & Goblet Co.

Greentown, Indiana

1894–1903

The glass commonly referred to as Greentown was actually manufactured by the Indiana Tumbler & Goblet Co. Indiana Tumbler began producing glassware in 1894 under the management of the Jenkins family, David C., Sr., David C., Jr., Thomas, and Lewis, Jr. In the trade paper of May 23, 1894, it was reported that:

> The Indiana Tumbler & Goblet Co. of this place, expect to be making glass not later than June 10. Their buildings are all of brick except the office, and of the following dimensions: Factory proper, 72 x 72 feet; packing room, 100 x 50 feet; mould shop, 52 x 46 feet; and barrel factory, 20 x 30 feet. The office is a frame building of three rooms located 25 feet from the main building and is finished in hard wood and otherwise conveniently arranged. When the plant is completed it will have a melting capacity of 18 pots; at present time there are one 10 pot furnace and four lears finished. They are going to make a full line of tumblers, beer mugs, jellies and stemware. The company have their own gas well right at the factory and have also 400 acres of gas land right in the heart of the Indiana field. They have secured the services of the best set of glassworkers that can be had and expect to give thorough satisfaction in regard to the material and workmanship of their product. This place is on the Clover Leaf R.R., one of the best roads in the state of Indiana. Everything about the factory is fitted up in the most thorough and effective manner, the equipments are as complete as the best skill and long experience in the business can make them, and the management is such as to secure the confidence of the trade from the start. Under these conditions the prospects of the new company for a prosperous future seem to be most favorable in all respects.

Their products included bar ware, jelly glasses, novelties and tableware. In 1897 the production of colored tableware began. In 1899 the firm became a part of the National Glass Co. and designated Factory #9 - Indiana Tumbler & Goblet Works. It should be noted that Chocolate Glass and Holly Amber were both manufactured under the National management. Jacob Rosenthal, who joined the firm in 1900, created the formula for Chocolate glass and sold it

Greentown Blue Glass Hen on Nest, 5.25 inches long, has wrong base. With correct base $185.

to National for use in their other glass works as well. His other formulas include Golden Agate and Rose Agate. The factory was destroyed by fire in June, 1903 and was not rebuilt. National Glass Company did continue some of its patterns.

Thanks to Bob Sanford for this information. For more visit gransplace.com.

Greentown? milk glass Robin on Nest covered dish. $125.

Greentown chocolate glass Hen on Nest, 5.25 inches long. $425.

Greentown milk glass Bird with Berry on split ribbed base. $325.

Greentown Glass chocolate glass Cat in Hamper. $250.

Greentown chocolate glass Dolphin covered dish, smooth edge around mouth. $200.

Greentown milk glass Rabbit covered dish; the bulging rim base is incorrect. With correct base, $165.

K. R. Haley Glassware Company

Greensburg, Pennsylvania

1939–1972

Kenneth Haley was the son of Reuben Haley and worked with him at Consolidated Glass from 1925 to 1928. He developed a friendship with Wal Przybylik and they continued to work on designs together for twenty years. K.R. Haley's career included stints at Phoenix Glass and the Overmeyer Mould Company in Greensburg, Pennsylvania. He established General Glassware Company in 1939, to market his designs, which were made by American Glass. A new company, K.R. Haley was formed in the early 1940s, closing in 1972 when Kenneth retired.

For more information about the company and other examples of their work see Debbie and Randy Coe's *Glass Figurines & Animals* (Schiffer, 2003). This was the source of much of the information in this brief essay.

K.R. Haley Glass Co., 1948, milk glass Prairie Schooner or Covered Wagon, 5.875 inches long; if perfect, $100.

Hazel Atlas Glass Company

Washington, Pennsylvania; Wheeling, West Virginia; Clarksburg, West Virginia

1902-1987

The Hazel Atlas Glass Company has its roots in a family of early 20th century industrialists in Pennsylvania and West Virginia. Three Brady brothers were each involved in leadership of manufacturing companies. Joseph C. Brady was made the Secretary and Manager of the Wheeling Hinge Company in 1880 and later founded the Wheeling Metal Company. Charles N. Brady was President of the Atlas Glass Company in Washington, Pennsylvania, and W.S. Brady was President of the Republic Glass Company in Clarksburg, West Virginia. In 1901 the four companies were merged into the Atlas Glass and Metal Company, under the leadership of the three brothers, Charles as President, W.S. as Vice President of operations, and Joseph as Secretary-Treasurer with responsibility for sales. Initial capitalization was $5,000.

Charles had formed another company, the Hazel Glass Company, in 1885 with Charles H. Tallman. It was the parent company of Atlas Glass Company, which was formed in 1896. Hazel made opal glass liners for Mason zinc caps.

In 1902 Hazel Glass joined Atlas Glass and Metal to form Hazel-Atlas Glass Company. The brothers continued in their leadership roles and the capitalization of the new company was $1,000,000.

Competition meant slow growth for the new company, but by 1930 they had expanded to five glass companies and a metal company. That same year they decided to move their headquarters to Wheeling, West Virginia, and erected a new building there. By 1956, when it became a division of the Continental Can Company, Hazel-Atlas had twelve glass manufacturing sites and its metal fabricating plant, including plants in California, New York, and Oklahoma. In 1964 Continental announced that the Wheeling headquarters would be sold. Six factories, producing primarily glass containers, were sold to Brockway Glass Company. In 1972 Brockway bought the Clarksburg tableware operation and continued to produce Hazel-Ware. In 1977 the Clarksburg plant was sold to Anchor Hocking, which closed it in 1982.

In 1936, Hazel-Atlas received a patent for Platonite, a white opaque color that they used in many of the novelty milk glass pieces they produced.

For more information you may visit the website of West Virginia Northern Community College at northern.wvnet.edu or gransplace.com. Pickvet's *The Encyclopedia of Glass* is also a useful resource. All of these were sources for the facts in this essay.

Hazel Atlas Hen on Basket, white on clear base., 4.5 inches. $28.

Hazel Atlas Hen on Basket, white., 4.5 inches. $28 each.

Imperial Glass Co.

Bellaire, Ohio

1901–1972

The Imperial Glass Co. was organized in 1901 by Edward Muhleman, J. N. Vance and James Anderson, and started operations in 1904. They advertised that their mould shop was making all new patterns. They started making colored glass in 1909. This was the most modern factory of its time. Their products included some art styles, milk glass, and colored pressed glass (Depression glass). The company briefly declared bankruptcy in 1929, but was able to continue operations. In 1940 they purchase Central Glass Works, and in 1958-59, when the Heisey and Cambridge factories closed, their moulds were purchased by Imperial. The Heisey moulds were later sold to the Heisey Collectors of America. Imperial Glass was purchased by Lenox in 1972 and continued to produce glass under the name of IGC Liquidating Corporation. It was then sold to Lancaster Colony Corporation, but glass production ceased.

Thanks to Bob Sanford for this information. For more information see *Milk Glass: Imperial Glass Corporation* by Myrna & Bob Garrison.

Imperial Hen on Basket, white 4.5 inches. $38.

Imperial purple slag Rooster on Open Lace Base. $60.

Imperial caramel Owl, 6.5 inches. $35.

Imperial Glass Grapes & Leaves sugar. $20.

Imperial green slag Owl jar, has original sticker. $50.

Imperial Duck on Basket covered dishes, green swirl, chocolate swirl, purple slag, and chocolate swirl, 4.5 inches. $38 each.

Imperial Duck on Basket, satin green swirl, 4.5 inches. $42.

Imperial Duck on Basket, white, 4.5 inches. $40.

Imperial purple swirl Duck covered dish. $55.

Imperial full body white Turkey, 5 inches. $40.

Imperial dark blue milk glass Atterbury-type covered Rabbit, marked IG, from the 1940s. $90.

Imperial Bunny on Nest covered dishes, white, 4.5 inches, ivory, 4.25 inches. $42 each.

1982 Imperial for Gurnsey black glass Rocking Horse #5, one of 12 made. $70.

Imperial purple slag Lion on Open Lace Base. $60.

Imperial Glass two-faced Owl toothpick. $25.

Imperial Glass Honey Jar. $28.

Imperial purple swirl Bee covered dish. $55.

Indiana Glass Co.

Dunkirk, Indiana

1904–2002

In 1904 The Indiana Glass Co. leased the National Glass Co. Glass works #1, the old Beatty-Brady Glass Company that National had purchased in 1899. Founded by Frank Merry, Henry Batsch, and others, they began operations using some moulds from the defunct #9 and #11 works of National. National went into receivership in 1907 and in 1908 Indiana purchased the factory and some of its moulds. This happened mostly because of the financial problems of National, which had put them into receivership. Production at first was mainly jelly glasses but after acquiring these moulds they started making tableware.

Thanks to Bob Sanford for this information.

Indiana Glass Hen on Nest, 7 inches. $30.

Jeannette Glass Company

Jeannette, Pennsylvania

1900–1983

Started in 1898 by Joseph Stoner, W.A. Huff, and others, it succeeded a bottle making operation, the Jeannette Bottle Works, which started in 1888. Glass was established in Jeannette, Pennsylvania in 1900. By 1927 they had automated production and were producing tableware and kitchen ware. Jeannette closed in 1983.

Jeannette divided pink milk glass covered dish, 6.5 inches. $125.

Kanawha Glass Company

Dunbar, West Virginia

1955–1987

Named after the nearby Kanawha River, the Kanawha Glass Specialties Co. was formed in 1955 in Dunbar, West Virginia. Among its founding members was D.P. Merritt production head of the defunct Dunbar Glass Co. They specialized in novelty and blown glass, and decorated pieces made by others. In 1957 their name was changed to Kanawha Glass Company. They purchased Hamon Handcrafted Glass, a Scott Depot, West Virginia, company in 1969. In the early 1970s Kanawha introduced cased milk glass, milk glass with a bright solid outer (or sometimes inner) layer. Kanawha was purchased by Raymond Dereume Glass Company of Punxsutawney, Pennsylvania in 1987, and production of its gift line was discontinued.

For more information on Kanawha Glass see Leslie Piña's *Crackle Glass in Color,* or visit gransplace.com. These sites were the primary sources for the facts in this essay.

Kanawha blue Hen on Basket. $32.

Kanawha blue Standing Rooster 10 inches tall. $28.

Kanawha blue satin Hen, 7.5 inches. $28.

Kemple Glass Company

East Palestine, Ohio • Kenova, West Virginia

1945–1970

A former employee of Fostoria, John E. Kemple founded his glass company in 1945. Specializing in moulded glass he began with moulds purchased from others including Co-operative Flint, Gillinder, McKee and others. These, along with mould purchased from failed glass operations, led to an inventory of over 1,100 glass moulds.

After a fire in 1956, the plant was moved to Kenova, West Virginia. Among their products were many milk and colored glass animal dishes, boxes, trays, and more. In 1970, when Kemple died, the moulds and equipment were sold to the Wheaton Glass Company, and the moulds are now part of the Wheaton Glass Museum in New Jersey.

To learn more see Pickvet's *Encyclopedia of Glass,* the source for these facts.

Kemple Hen on Nest, pink milk glass, 7 inches. $28.

Kemple milk glass Chicken. $50.

Pair of Kemple milk glass Rooster bookends, 8 inches tall, original stickers. $45 each.

Kemple milk glass Dove on Split Rib Base. $40.

Kemple milk glass Turkey on Split Rib Base. $40.

Kemple milk glass Turkey. $50.

Kemple satin glass Turkey on Split Rib Base. $32.

Kemple milk glass Cow covered dish, 8 inches. $90 each.

Kemple milk glass Lamb on Split Rib Base. $50.

Kemple Indian Head toothpick or matchholder, 3.25 inches tall. $25.

MacBeth-Evans Glass Company

Charleroi, Pennsylvania

1899–?

George MacBeth and Thomas Evans joined forces in 1899 to form the MacBeth-Evans Glass Company. Evans had helped found the Reddick Glass Company in Pittsburgh in 1869 and later established the Crescent Glass Works. MacBeth was in on the founding of Keystone Flint Glass Works in Pittsburgh in 1872, later founding Geo. A. MacBeth and Company in the old Atterbury White House plant. In the 1890s, both established factories in Indiana. After the merger they moved from a hand operation to a pressed glass business. In 1936 Corning bought the company and the factory in Charleroi is still in operation.

MacBeth Evans Co. milk glass Swan Song vase, 5.5 inches wide. $65.

McKee & Bros.

Pittsburgh, PA. • Jeannette, PA.

1835–1951

The first McKee glass factory was S. McKee & Co. and was established on the South Side of Pittsburgh in 1835 by Thomas McKee and his brother Samuel, for the manufacture of green bottle goods. Frederick, Stuart, and William McKee, sons of Thomas, organized McKee & Bros and built a flint glass factory at South Eighteenth Street. H. Sellers McKee, a younger brother, was a clerk in the firm. Later Thomas sold his interest in S. McKee & Co. and joined his sons at McKee & Bros. Thomas (the father) died in 1866 and H. Sellers became a partner in McKee & Bros. H. Sellers acquired most of the holdings of his brothers and in 1884, when his brother Stuart died, he was the largest owner of stock in the firm. When their South Eighteenth Street property was acquired by the Pittsburg & Lake Erie Railroad a new plant was erected and put into operation at Jeannette, Pennsylvania in 1892. A. Hart McKee, son of H. Sellers, became a partner and the name McKee & Bros. was continued. In 1899 the company became part of the National Glass Company. In 1904 the National Glass Co. retired from manufacturing and leased its properties. The McKee & Bros. glass works were leased to a chartered firm of McKee-Jeannette Glass Co. There was no involvement by the McKee family in the new firm.

This company was known for its manufacture of tableware, stemware, lamps and novelties. From 1897 to 1902 they manufactured many novelties and covered animal dishes in milk glass, but as the 20th century progressed they moved in to industrial glass. In 1951 McKee became a division of Thatcher Glass Company and sold nearly 300 original moulds to John E. Kemple Glass. Thatcher continued to use the McKee name until 1961, when they were sold to Jeannette Glass Company.

Thanks to Bob Sanford for the bulk of this information. It was augmented by Pickvet's *Encyclopedia of Glass.*

McKee milk glass Hen on Nest covered dish, unsigned. $180.

McKee milk glass Hen on Nest with Chick covered dish, split ribbed base, unsigned. $150.

McKee Chick double head, top signed. $900.

McKee milk glass Rooster on Nest covered dish, top signed. $200.

McKee milk glass Owl Head covered dish, split ribbed base, unsigned. $250.

McKee milk glass Swan covered dish, signed top. $185.

McKee milk glass Dove covered dish, unsigned, split ribbed base. $150.

McKee milk glass Duck covered dish, signed base. $475.

McKee Canary covered dish on Basket Weave Base, top signed. $600.

McKee Cow covered dish, signed base. $950.

McKee milk glass Cat covered dish, signed top. $160.

McKee Elephant covered dish, unsigned, split rib base. $1800.

McKee milk glass Dog covered dish, top signed, split ribbed base. $325.

McKee milk glass Rabbit covered dish, unsigned, basket weave base. $65.

McKee milk glass Rabbit covered dish, unsigned. $175.

McKee milk glass Squirrel covered dish, signed top and bottom. $475.

McKee milk glass Horse covered dish, signed top, top has a red tint to it. $225.

McKee milk glass Lion covered dish, signed top, split ribbed base. $200.

McKee Pig covered dish, piece is unsigned, split rib base. $1350.

McKee milk glass Frog covered dish, split ribbed base, unsigned. $375.

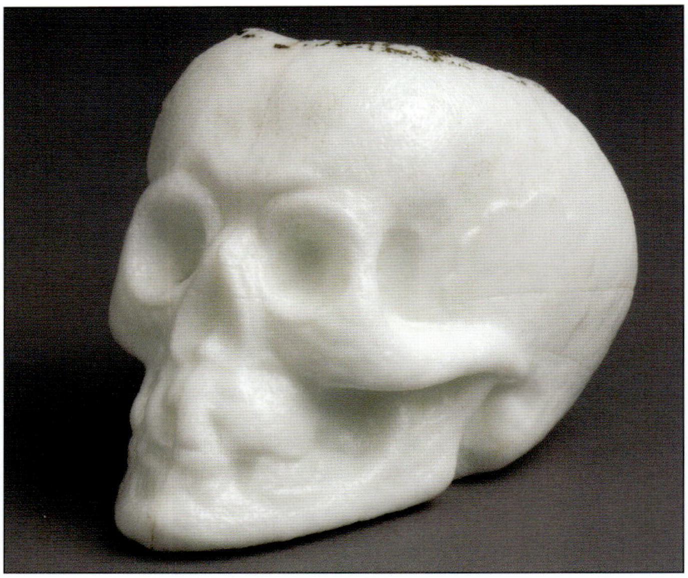

McKee Ramses III toothpick. $250.

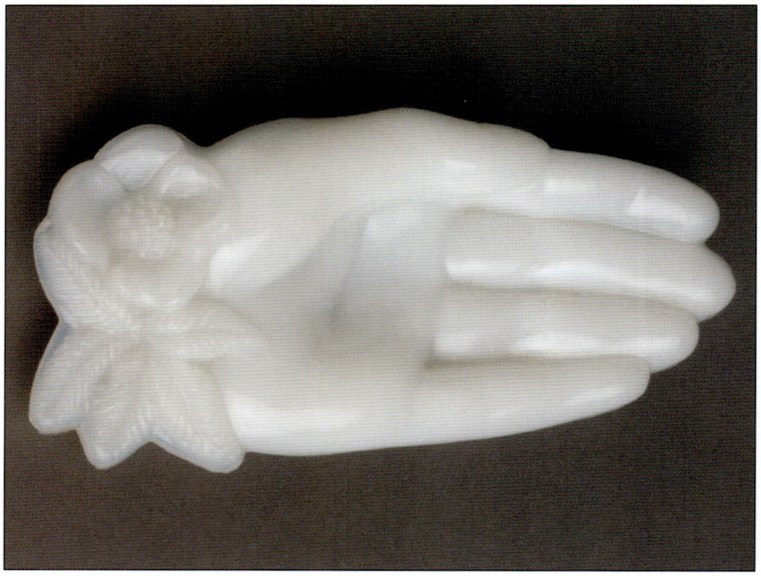

McKee milk glass Hand. $175.

McKee card holder with Heart. $45.

McKee milk glass Bird House with yellow top, new bottom. $80.

McKee milk glass Yachting Cap signed. $175

McKee Straw Hat. $150.

Mosser Glass Company

Cambridge Ohio

1971–Present

Thomas Mosser grew up in the glass industry. His father, Orie, was a plant manager at Cambridge Glass Company, and Thomas worked there after school and in the summers as a teenager. It was great training. Committed to making quality glass, he gathered together the equipment and moulds he needed and started Variety Glass in 1959, opening his workshop in a chicken coop.

The company concentrated on pharmaceutical glassware and built a strong reputation for quality which led to its growing success. In 1971 he founded Mosser Glass which continues today as a family firm with 30 people involved in the glassmaking process. They develop new designs as well as keeping classics from Viking, L.G. Wright, and Cambridge alive.

Mosser Glass is known for its miniatures, novelty items and tablewares, as well as industrial, pharmaceutical, and scientific glass.

The company website is at mosserglass.com. Additonal information came from Pickvet's *Encyclopedia of Glass.*

Mosser Hen on Nest, with red head. $28.

Mosser milk glass Sleigh. $28.

Rosso Wholesale Glass Dealers, Inc.

Port Vue, Pennsylvania

c. 1960–Present

The roots of Rosso Glass lie in the interests of Helen and Phil Rosso. In the early 1960s they began collecting glass and, by the early 1970s, they were buying glassware for resale. Westmoreland Glass provided many of these items, and in 1983 when Westmoreland went out of business, the Rossos bought inventory and seventy-five moulds. In 1988 they moved the company and started the Westmoreland Museum with almost 5000 pieces of 20th century glass. Rosso uses some of the Westmoreland moulds, as well as moulds from other companies, to have glass made, though they do not make it themselves. Work has been done by Mosser, Fenton, Summit, and L.E. Smith.

For more information on Rosso, visit their company website wholesale-glass-dealer.com or gransplace.com.

Rosso purple slag Rooster, 9 inches tall. $32.

David Schepps

Salem, New Jersey

David Schepps is a renowned frog collector from Salem, New Jersey. He has designed several glass moulds in the frog motif. This mould was made by Quality Mold of Latrobe, Pennsylvania. Some of Schepps pieces, including this one are manufactured by Boyd Glass.

Schepps pink Frog on Base, 5.5 inches. $50.

L.E. Smith

Jeannette, Pennsylvania

1907–Present

Still in operation today, L.E. Smith Glass was started in 1907, by Lewis E. Smith, a mustard maker in search of the a good container, and Thomas Twible. They began in Jeannette as a glass decorating firm, but soon purchased a glass factory in Mt. Pleasant, Pennsylvania and began glass manufacturing. Smith left the company in 1911, though his name continues to identify the company. Fire brought about a new building in Mt. Pleasant and growth meant an additional factory in Greensburg, Pennsylvania. Their products included novelty glass, utilitarian glass, tablewares, and some automotive lighting. In 1976 they were purchased by Owens-Illinois and continue operating as L.E. Smith today.

L.E. Smith Scottie Dog, 5 in. $35.

L.E. Smith Open Swan, 9 inches wide. $25.

L.E. Smith milk glass Cinderella's Coaches, 6.5 inches long and 5 inches long. $25-40 each.

Three Glass Slippers, light blue Daisy & Button, dark blue Daisy & Button and white L.E. Smith. $10 each.

Summit Art Glass

Akron, Ohio • Rootsville, Ohio

1972–2004

Summit Art Glass was founded in 1972 by Russell and Joanne Vogelsang. They are known for their colored and milk glass reproduction using moulds of now defunct companies, including Cambridge, Westmoreland, Imperial, St. Clair and Tiffin, though they sometimes did so in colors that were unique. They also made some art and novelty glass of their own design. Most pieces carry the Summit mark, though certain dealers would rather you did not look for it on some of the reproduction pieces; some pieces known to be Summit are unmarked. Trademarks include a block letter S, a V in a circle, and a hand over an oval with the words "handpressed in the U.S.A./Summit Art Glass. Summit suspended operations in 2004.

For more information see Pickvet's *Encyclopedia of Glass,* and www.gransplace.com. Both were used as sources for this information.

Summit Horse on Split Rib Base. $30.

Summit yellow marble Lion, 4.75 inches. $25.

Vallerystahl • Portieux • PV France

Alsace-Lorraine, France

1836–Present

The history here is a bit fuzzy. Two companies, Vallerystahl and Portieux, have their roots in the early 1700s in the Alsace-Lorraine area of France. Vallerystahl was founded in 1836 and joined with the Portieux factory some 60 miles away under a single management in 1854. Under German occupation, the companies separated to be rejoined in 1872 as the "Limited Society of Amalgamated Glass Makers of Vallerystahl and Portieux."

Among their products was a line of milk glass animal dishes. According to *Yesterday's Milk Glass Today,* by Regis and Mary Ferson, the company began exporting a significant number of milk glass pieces in the 1870s and continued until interrupted by World War I around 1914.

Debbie Coe reports (kaleden.com) that Vallerystahl and Portieux acquired some moulds from a mouldmaker in Pittsburgh, which may account for some of the similarity in form. The French glass, however, is distinguishable from American glass by its gray "tinge," and by the fact that it is not as dense as the American version.

For more information see the Ferson's book, self-published in 1981, or visit kalenden.com

Vallerystahl Hen on Nest. 5.5 inches, both painted. $110.

Vallerystahl Hen on Nest. 6 inches, painted. $110.

Vallerysthal blue milk glass Hen on Basket Base, 7.25 x 8.75 inches, deep nest piece. $215.

Vallerysthal green milk glass Hen on Basket Base, 7.25 x 8.75 inches, deep nest piece. $215.

Vallerysthal milk glass blue Hen on Nest, 5.5 inches long. $95.

Seven Vallerystahl Hens on Nests, 2.5 inches to 7 inches. $60 (2.5 inches) to $110 (large).

Vallerysthal milk glass breakfast set including bottom tray and six egg cups, Hen is marked, set is missing one piece that goes in front of hen. $225.

Two Vallerysthal Duck open salts, blue and white milk glass. $40 each.

Two Vallerystahl Swimming Ducks, one blue, one white, 5 inches. $150 each.

Vallerysthal milk glass Duck, 6.75 inches long. $70.

Vallerysthal milk glass Ducks. Left: 6.75 inches long; right: 5 inches long. $70 each.

Vallerysthal blue milk glass Robin on Nest, covered dish, 5 inches long. $80

Vallerysthal blue milk glass Open Neck Swan covered dish, unsigned. $85.

Vallerysthal blue milk glass Duck 5 inches long covered dish. $75.

Vallerysthal blue milk glass Rabbit on Egg covered dish, unsigned. $160.

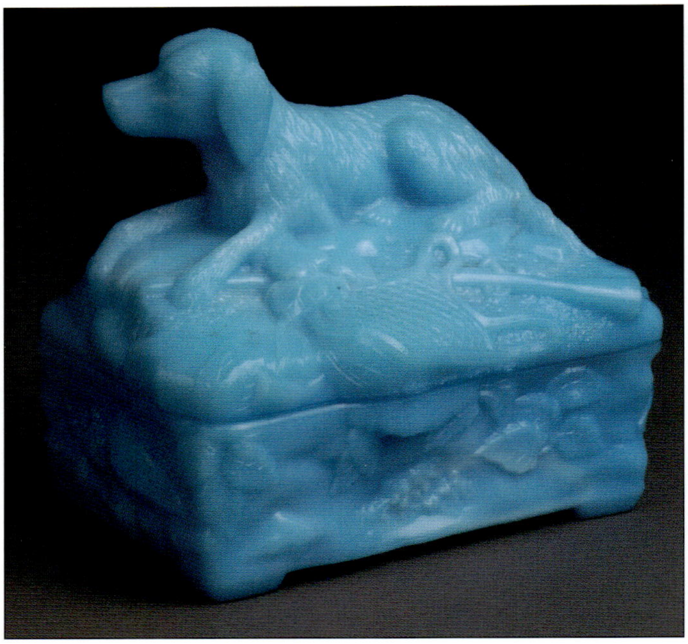

Vallerysthal blue milk glass Setter Dog on Rug with Gun covered dish. $150.

Vallerysthal Dog on a Rug covered dish, not signed. $150.

Rare Vallerysthal caramel glass Dog on Rug, signed based. $1050.

Vallerysthal yellow glass Dog on Steamer Rug with Floral Base covered dish, unsigned. $90.

Vallerysthal blue milk glass Elephant with Rider covered dish, unsigned, gold painted head and trunk. $130.

Vallerysthal blue milk glass Dog On Steamer Rug with Floral Base covered dish, unsigned. $95.

Vallerysthal blue Setter. $150.

Vallerysthal blue milk glass Fish covered dish, signed base. $375.

Vallerysthal blue milk glass Snail on Strawberry covered dish, unsigned. $85.

Vallerysthal blue milk glass Snail on Turtle covered dish. $425.

Vallerysthal milk glass Rabbit on Egg covered dishes. $65 each.

Vallerysthal milk glass Squirrel on Acorn. $80.

Vallerysthal milk glass Snail on Strawberry covered dish. $75.

Vallerysthal milk glass Squirrel on Fancy Base covered dish. $120.

Vallerysthal blue milk glass Squirrel atop lid on Fancy Base, unsigned. $80.

Vallerysthal blue milk glass Squirrel on Acorn covered dish. $85.

Vallerysthal Reclining Cow covered dish, has some of the original paint. $300.

Vallerysthal blue covered footed sugar, 6 inches. $65.

Vallerysthal blue Egg Service Set, C/S 364. $125.

Vallerysthal blue milk glass Cabbage covered dish, unsigned. $100.

Vallerysthal blue milk glass Lemon sugar bowl. $425.

Vallerysthal green milk glass Melon covered dish, signed on base. $90.

Vallerysthal milk glass Cabbage covered dish. $95.

Vallerysthal? Beehive covered dish, 5 x 4.25 inches. $45.

Vallerysthal? Beehive with Vines covered dish, unsigned, 5.5 x 4.25 inches. $48.

Portieux blue milk glass Standing Rooster covered dish, base signed, painted comb, wings & tail. $100.

Portieux green milk glass Standing Rooster covered dish, base signed. $100.

Portieux milk glass Standing Rooster covered dish, base signed, top has original paint faded a bit. $100.

Portieux milk glass Standing Rooster covered dish, base signed. $100.

Portieux Robin on Pedestal. $85.

Portieux blue milk glass Cat on Drum. $140.

Portieux blue milk glass Rabbit covered dish, 7 inches long. $250.

Portieux milk glass Rabbit covered dish, 7 inches long. $250.

Portieux pink glass Rabbit covered dish, 7 inches long. $250.

Portieux blue Pig on Drum. Left: pink satin glass; center: blue milk glass with gold highlights; right: white milk glass. All colors $150-195.

Blue Portieux Turtle salt. $185.

Portieux green milk glass "The Hunter" match holder, signed. $175.

Portieux Cat on Drum covered dish, one white. $125.

Portieux milk glass Old Man with Basket, signed. $150 each.

Portieux Picnic Basket. $125.

Portieux white milk glass Cannon on Drum. $125.

PV France blue milk glass Hen on Nest. $60.

PV France blue milk glass Hens on Nests, 4 x 5.5 inches. $40 each.

Two PV France green milk glass Hens on Nests, small one has label, 4 x 4 inches; larger one no label, 4 x 5.5 inches. $75 each.

PV France Blue milk glass Standing Rooster. $75.

PV France blue milk glass Dog on Streamer Rug with Floral Base, with sticker. $90.

PV France blue milk glass Pineapple covered dish, 7 inches tall. $40.

Westmoreland Specialty Company (WSC) • *Westmoreland Glass Company*

Grapeville, Pa.

1889–1984

The Westmoreland Specialty Company (WSC) traced it roots to 1889, when a group of investors from the Specialty Glass Company in East Liverpool, Ohio, led by A.J. Stevenson, migrated to Grapeville, Pennsylvania, drawn by its abundance of natural gas. They built a new factory in the fall of 1889, along with room for workers to move their families to the area. In 1890 glass production began. Among the founding employees were brothers George and Charles West, who, with the help of financier Ira Brainard, purchased the company from Stevenson and Specialty Glass, forming Westmoreland Specialty Company in the early 1890s. The brothers successfully ran the company until 1920 when they had a falling out, and George sold his interest Charles and Brainard. The name was changed to Westmoreland Glass Company in 1923. During the Depression the Brainard family bought the remaining interest in the company from Charles, and established James J. Brainard as president. His son, James H. succeeded him in 1953, with another son, Walter M., as vice president. In 1981 the company was sold to Dave Grossman, and in 1984 it was closed.

During the 1940s and 1950s the company produced vast amounts of milk glass and other opaque glass. James H. Brainard once estimated milk glass production as being 90% of the total output during this period.

There are active groups of Westmoreland collectors around the world. For more information visit westmorelandglassclubs.org. Their website along with Pickvet's *Encyclopedia of Glass* were the source for the information in this brief essay.

WSC black glass and amber glass Hen on Nest covered dish with white heads; label on black glass figure. $125 each.

WSC blue milk glass Hen on Nest. $55.

WSC blue milk glass Hen with white head. $80.

Two WSC Hen on Nest covered dishes, black with white head and amber with white head. $125 each.

WSC dark blue milk glass Hen on Nest with white head and light blue Hen on Nest. $65.

WSC Hen on Nest covered dish, white with some paint. $45.

WSC Hen on Nest covered dish, white with blue head and base. $50.

WSC light blue milk glass Hen on Nest with white head and Hen with light base, dark top with white head. $60.

WSC milk glass Hen on Nest covered dish. $50.

WSC milk glass Chicken on Basket covered dishes. $15-25 each.

WSC milk glass Chicken on Basket, some paint. $85.

WSC milk glass Chicken on Sleigh, some paint. $45.

WSC milk glass Emerging Chick on Basket, some paint. $45.

WSC milk glass Round Basket of Emerging Chicks covered dishes. $40.

WSC milk glass Emerging Chick on Sleigh, some paint. $45.

WSC milk glass Emerging Chick on sleigh. $45.

WSC blue milk glass Rooster with white head. $45 each.

WSC milk glass Rooster on blue base, white top with blue head. $60.

WSC milk glass Rooster & Hen on Nest covered dishes with blue heads. $50 each.

WSC milk glass Rooster with some paint. $50.

WSC milk glass Closed Neck Swan covered dish; has trace of gold paint. $85.

WSC blue Closed Neck Swan covered dish. $85.

WSC blue Swan on Cattails creamer & sugar. $68 set

WSC blue milk glass Pin Tail Duck covered dish. $60.

WSC milk glass Pintail Duck covered dish with some paint. $50.

WSC milk glass Pintail Duck covered dish. $45.

WSC milk glass Rabbit on Picket Base covered dish. $60.

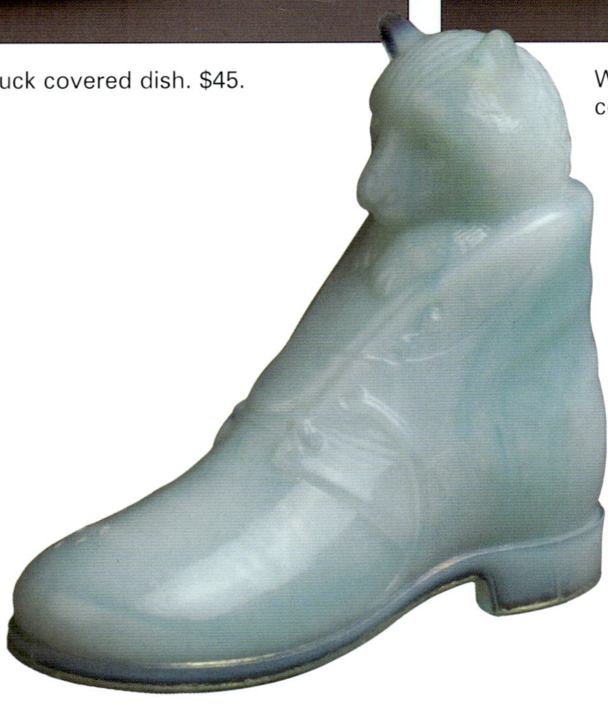

WSC Cat in Boot. $100.

WSC milk glass Cats, one blue with white head and one in white milk glass. $60 each.

WSC milk glass Dog covered dish, blue top with white head on white base. $60.

WSC milk glass Lamb covered dish. $65.

WSC milk glass Lamb on Picket Base covered dish. $65.

WSC Lamb on Picket Base covered dish, blue with white head. $65.

WSC milk glass Lion on Picket Base and blue Lion on Picket base with white head. $60.

WSC milk glass Log Cabin Bank. $185.

WSC milk glass Lover steins. $35 each.

WSC milk glass Robed Santa on Sleigh. $110.

WSC milk glass School House Bank. $185.

WSC Owl paper weight. $125.

WSC milk glass. $50.

WSC milk glass Uncle Sam Hat with paint. $65.

WSC Painted milk glass School House mustard/ bank, has original sticker on bottom. $185.

Two Westmoreland Glass Hen on Basket covered dishes. $38.

Red slag Rooster on Base, marked Westmoreland Made by Summit, 7.5 inches. $30.

Westmoreland Glass "Welcome Home Westmoreland" painted hen. $55.

Westmoreland Glass white Hen on Nest with Eggs, 7.25 inches. $35.

Westmoreland Glass white with red head Hen on Nest with Eggs, 7.25 inches. $50.

Westmoreland Glass caramel Standing Rooster, 9 inches. $40.

Westmoreland Glass Chick on Pile of Eggs, painted, 6.5 inches. $40.

Westmoreland Glass Standing Rooster covered dish. $50 each.

Chocolate Eagle with Chicks, marked "Westmoreland Made by Summit." $32.

Chocolate Chick on Pile of Eggs, marked "Westmoreland Made by Summit." $32.

Three Westmoreland Swan & Cattails creamers. $38 each.

Westmoreland Glass Swan on Open Lacy Base covered dish, 10 inches. $60.

Westmoreland Three Swan toothpick. $32.

Westmoreland Glass white Duck on Base, 8 inches diameter. $50 if marked Westmoreland; if not, then Challinor, $175

Westmoreland Glass duck toothpicks. $40 each.

Unmarked Welcome Home Westmoreland Duck on Wavy Base and Duck on Wavy Base, maker unknown, 8 inches. $38 each.

Westmoreland Glass blue Robin on Pedestal Nest covered dishes, 5 inches diameter. $45.

Westmoreland Glass white Robin on Pedestal Nest, 5 inches diameter. $45.

Westmoreland Glass Wren on a Perch. $65.

Westmoreland Glass light blue Mother Eagle on Lacy Base covered dish, 8.5 inches. $70.

Westmoreland Glass Mother Eagle covered dish. $65.

Westmoreland Glass Love Birds on Base, 6 inches. $55.

Westmoreland Glass mark.

Westmoreland Glass Love Birds on Base covered dishes, 6 inches. $55 each.

Westmoreland Glass Dolphin and Shell sugar bowls. $45 each.

Two Westmoreland Glass Pigs. $42 each.

Chocolate Horse on Base, marked "Westmoreland Made by Summit," 7.5 inches. $32.

Westmoreland Glass blue Resting Camel covered dish, 6.5 inches. $100.

Westmoreland Glass white Resting Camel. $65.

Westmoreland Glass Fox on Lacy Base, painted. $45.

Westmoreland Glass milk glass Fox on Lacy Base. $45.

Westmoreland Glass white Rabbit on Base covered dish. $65.

Westmoreland Glass purple slag glass Rabbit on Base covered dish. $65.

Westmoreland Glass Rabbit on Grass, 5.5 inches. $40.

Westmoreland Glass Rabbit with Painted Eggs, 7 inches. $40.

Westmoreland Glass Lamb on Base, painted. $65.

Westmoreland Glass purple slag Lion on Basket, 7.5 inches. $85.

Westmoreland Tyrolean Bear jar, round. $125.

Very rare Imperial caramel slag Pie Wagon with original stickers, marked AIG on bottom. $150.

Westmoreland Glass light blue and milk glass Cat on Lacy Base covered dishes, 8.5 inches. $90.

Two Westmoreland Glass Picnic Baskets, white and green. $35 each.

Westmoreland Chubby creamer & sugar, 4.875 inches. $45 set

Westmoreland Cornucopia, blue and white, 5.5 inches. $68 set

Westmoreland Glass Open Hands dish. $70.

Westmoreland Glass Santa on Sleigh. $35.

Westmoreland Glass scalloped dish. $55.

Westmoreland Glass blue Open Lace compote. $65.

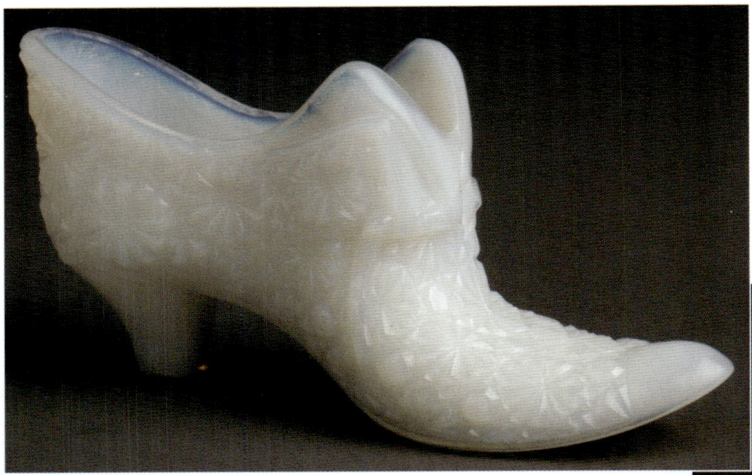

Westmoreland Glass Shoe, Daisy and Button. $38.

Westmoreland Glass Shoe, beading across toe. $38.

Westmoreland Glass Shoe, painted flowers. $38.

Westmoreland Glass Straw Hat ashtray. $30.

L.G. Wright

New Martinsville, West Virginia

1937–1999

In 1936, Lawrence Gale Wright, a traveling salesman, became the rep for his hometown glass company, New Martinsville Glass, along with other Midwest glass and pottery companies, including Paden City Pottery, Cumbow China Decorating, Westmoreland Glass, and others. By 1937 the L.G. Wright Company was founded as a marketing and development firm. Wright acquired moulds both from defunct glass companies and from mould makers, then had them manufactured by other glass firms. These included Fenton, Imperial, Paden City, Viking, Cambridge, and Westmoreland. For a more complete list see *L.G. Wright Glass,* by The West Virginia Museum of American Glass, Ltd. (Schiffer, 2003). The use of existing moulds led to the confusion of many Wright pieces with the originals. In 1974, L.G. Wright added their trademark to the pieces they produced.

L.G. Wright died in 1969, with his wife, Verna Mae, taking over the operation of the company. After her death the company passed over to a cousin, Dorothy Stephan and her daughter Phyllis Stephan Beuttner. The company continued until 1999.

For more information, including most useful lists of the companies that produced Wright's glass and of the purchasers of the moulds at the companies auction in 1999, see *L.G. Wright Glass,* by the West Virginia Museum of American Glass (Schiffer, 2003). The WVMAG holds the company archives in their collection. They are the source for many of the facts shared above.

L.G. Wright caramel Hen on Nest, 5.5 inches. $35.

L.G. Wright caramel swirl Hen on Basket. $40.

L.G. Wright custard Hen and Chicks on Basket, 5.5 inches. $40.

L.G. Wright light purple slag Hen with Eggs on Basket, 7.25 inches. $45.

L.G. Wright purple slag Hen on Basket, 4 inches. $45.

L.G. Wright purple slag Hen on Basket, 5.5 inches. $35.

L.G. Wright purple slag Rooster on Basket, 5.5 inches. $35.

L.G. Wright purple slag Rooster on Basket. $40.

L.G. Wright purple slag Hen with Eggs on Basket, 7.25 inches. $40.

L.G. Wright purple slag Turkey on Basket, 5.5 inches. $35.

L.G. Wright blue Swan on Basket. $45.

L.G. Wright purple slag Swan on Basket, 5.5 inches. $35.

L.G. Wright blue milk glass Atterbury-type Duck covered dish with white head. $25.

L.G. Wright Atterbury-type Ducks. $30 each.

L.G. Wright amethyst body and white head, Duck on Flange Base. $45.

L.G. Wright caramel slag Owl Head on BAsket, 5.5 inches. $35.

L.G. Wright custard Owl Head on BAsket, 5.5 inches. $35.

L.G. Wright orange slag Owl Head on Basket, 5.5 inches. $35.

L.G. Wright blue slag Cow on Basket, 5.5 inches. $35.

L.G. Wright blue swirl Cow on Basket. $40.

L.G. Wright purple slag Bull Head Mustard, no ladle. $40.

L.G. Wright purple slag Cat
on Basket, 5.5 inches. $35.

L.G. Wright purple slag Dog on Basket, 5.5 inches. $35.

L.G. Wright purple slag Horse on Basket, 5.5 inches. $35.

L.G. Wright large, full- body Snapping Turtle. $100.

L.G. Wright purple slag Lamb on Basket, 5.5 inches. $35.

R. & G.A. Wright

Philadelphia, Pennsylvania

c. 1860-1870

The R. & G.A. Wright Company, of Philadelphia, had a store at 624 Chestnut and a laboratory on Cypress Street, and was a manufacturer of perfumery and an importer of fancy goods, & druggist's sundries.

R&GA Wright milk glass Bear jar, 5.25 inches tall, marked on base. $600.

Miscellaneous Milk Glass

Covered Dishes & Bowls

Hen on Nest. $42.

Milk glass Hen with Eggs on Basket, 7.25 inches, maker unknown. $60.

Chocolate swirl Hen on Basket covered dish, 6 inches. $42.

Emerging Chick on Easter Egg Base covered dish. $38.

Milk glass Square Basket with Chicks covered dish. $800.

Milk glass White Hen with Eggs on Basket covered dish, 5.25 inches. $42.

Large Polish milk glass Hen on Nest covered dish. $95.

Two Czech Hen on Basket covered dishes, blue and jade, 5.75 inches. $38 each.

Milk glass ovoid Duck covered dish, 5 inches long, top marked SV. $45.

Painted Rooster covered dish, 7.5 inches wide. $20.

Milk glass Duck on rush base covered dish. $100.

Blue Duck covered dish, 5 inches. $250.

Swan on Water Base covered dish, maker unknown, 7.5 inches. $40.

Milk glass Birds in Kerchief covered dish, made in Finland. $60.

Purple slag Robin on Nest covered dish. $65.

Slag marbled Cat on Base covered dish. $42.

Green milk glass Dove covered dish. $60.

Slag marbled Horse on Base covered dish. $44.

Milk glass Cow on Wooden Tub Base covered dish. $175 rare

Left: Rabbit on Wide Rib Base covered dish, green body, white head; Rabbit on Ribbed Base, white with green head. $400+ each.

Full body purple slag Rabbit covered dish. $65.

Chocolate milk glass Rabbit covered dish, 7.25 inches, maker unknown. $42.

Dolphin covered dish in blue milk glass. $38.

Milk glass British Lion covered dish. $150.

Slag marbled Dolphin covered dish. $32.

Milk glass Flat Fish covered dish. $125.

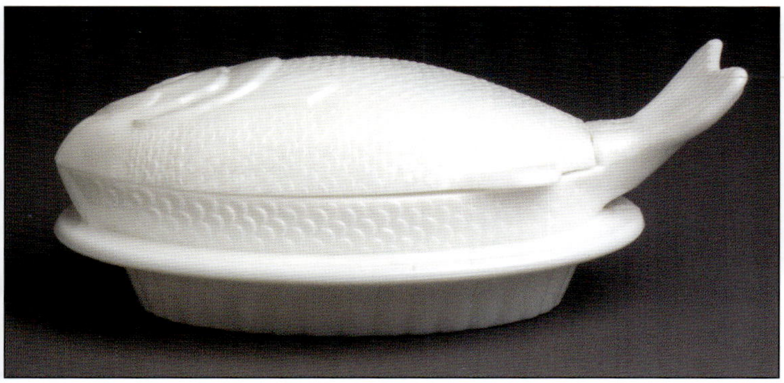

Brown slag glass Dolphin covered bowl. $60.

Shell covered dishes, with sticker. $65.

Melon covered dish. $75.

Basket with Apple Top covered bowl. $60.

Pink milk glass covered bowl in leaf pattern. $35.

White milk glass covered bowl in fruit motif, some remnants of paint. $60.

Milk glass Moses in the Bulrushes on raised top of covered dishes on Rush Bottoms. $500.

Closed Capstan Battleship Maine covered dish. $50.

Pope Leon covered dish, 5.5 inches. $100.

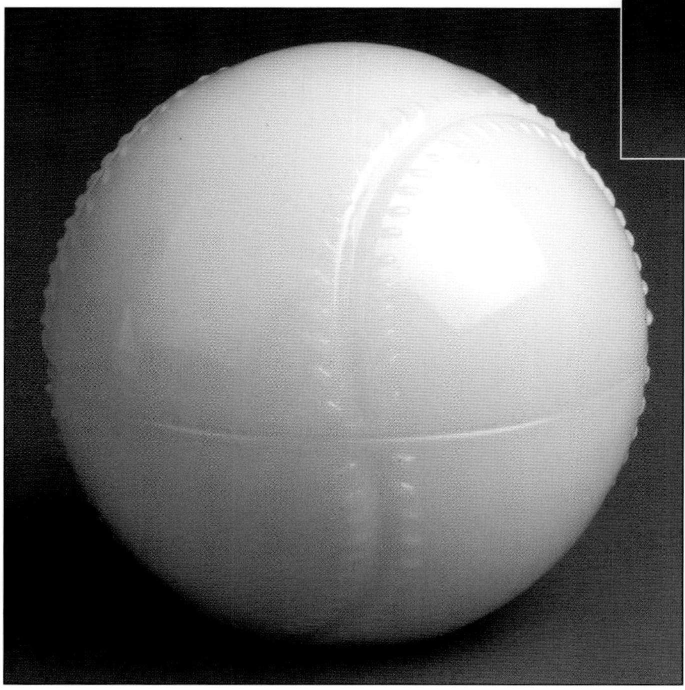

Milk glass Baseball covered dish. $85.

Milk glass Football on Pedestal covered dish. $85.

Green milk glass Crown covered dish, has British mark on bottom, 3.5 x 4 inches, top is rough around the rim. $550.

Covered pedestal dish. $38.

Blue milk glass covered bowl. $42.

Small covered dish, fading paint, 4 inches wide. $28.

Blue milk glass covered bowls. $55.

Jars

Chick on a Basket condiment jar. $65.

Milk glass Owl jar missing lid. $450-500 if complete.

Milk glass "Old Abe" covered jar. $200.

Milk glass Easter Rabbit Emerging from Top of Egg covered jar. $80.

Ear of Corn condiment Jar. $65.

Three Oriental Tea jars, two with a boy and one with a girl, various conditions and paint. $68 each.

Milk glass Queen Victoria covered jar. $65.

Covered marmalade jar. $48.

Open Dishes and Bowls

Milk glass Car candy container. $95.

Zipper & Bead nappy. $48.

Small blue milk glass bowl. $38.

Square green milk glass bowl with scalloped feet and small tab handle. $42.

Blue milk glass Barrel. $85.

Scalloped milk glass bowl with cherry motif. $45.

Milk glass open oval bowl. $25.

Blue milk glass bowl. $38.

Compotes

Blue swirl milk glass covered compote, 8.5 inches. $42.

Milk glass compote. $48.

Swirled Compote. $35.

Little Red Hen plate with faded paint. $48.

Chick & Egg tray. $42.

Chicks plate. $32.

Easter Ducks plate. $38.

Three Owls plate, 7.5 inches, fading paint. $55.

Flag and Eagle plate, 7.5 inches. $38.

Owl Lovers plate. $35.

Eagle, Flags, and Star plate. $45.

Blue Three Bears plate. $32.

Three Bears plate, 7.5 inches, fading paint. $32.

Three Bears plate, painted, 7.5 inches. $32.

Three Bears plate 7.5 inches. $32.

Woof Woof plate, 7.5 inches. $32.

Milk glass Three Kittens plate, 7.5 inches. $25.

Easter Bunny & Egg plate with faded paint. $35.

Three Kittens plate, 7.5 inches, faded paint. $25.

Easter Rabbits plate, 7.5 inches. $38.

Rabbit plate 7.5 inches. $35.

Cupid plate, 7.5 inches, fading paint. $42.

Contrary Mule plate. $38.

Cupid plate. $42.

Horseshoe plate. $65.

Round plate with painted Forget-Me-Not pierced rim and chick painting. $38.

Plate with grapevine border, not pierced. $25.

Ivy plate with club-pierced gothic arch rim. $28.

Niagara Falls plate. $38.

Club, Shell and Loop Border plate with image of the US Battleship Maine. $28.

Round blue plate with backward C-pierced rim. $38.

Square plate with pierced "S" rim. $38.

Round blue plate with pierced Keyhole Variant rim. $38.

Round, deep plate with block rim. $42.

Heart-shaped plate with pierced heart rim. $30.

Apple-shaped plate. $20.

Fleur de Lys plate, 7.5 inches. $32.

Basket plate with lace edge. $25.

Milk glass mug, 6.5 inches. $45.

Child's mug. $38.

Blue milk glass mug. $45.

White milk glass Barrel mug. $30.

Child's mug. $38.

Blue milk glass goblet, 4.5 inches. $25.

Pink marbled slag glass tumbler. $250+

Painted milk glass tumbler, 4 inches. $48.

Two pink milk glass footed tumblers, 6 inches. $22 each.

St. Louis World's Fair tumbler, 5 inches high. $55.

Cherries milk glass creamer. $25.

Pear covered sugar. $38.

Woman figural milk glass syrup. $65.

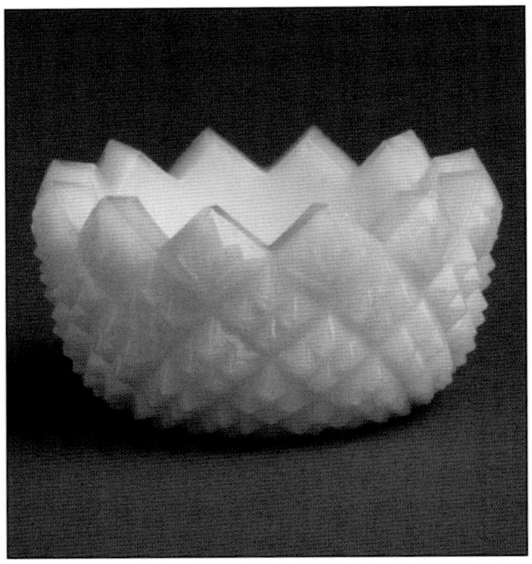

Small milk glass creamer and sugar. $20 each.

Strawberry milk glass syrup. $125.

Two blue milk glass creamers. $35 each.

Small pitcher. $45.

Roman Cross milk glass creamer. $38.

Blue milk glass carafe. $38.

Blue milk glass water pitcher. $65.

E.G. Booz's Old Cabin Whiskey milk glass decanter. $50.

Americana Boston Tea Party milk glass decanter. $65.

Reverse and stopper of Americana Boston Tea Party decanter.

Eye Opener Flask. $75.

Shakers

Three Bee Hive shakers. $575.

Refrigerator covered box. $250.

Milk glass Refrigerator shakers. $45 pair

Milk glass shakers in grapevine pattern. $38 each.

Blue milk glass shakers. $48.

Salt and Pepper Shakers, pair of Chicks. $110.

Open Salts

Milk glass Hen double salt, marked SV in one basket. 2.25 x 3.75 inches. $250.

Blue milk glass Dog with Baskets salt, marked SV in one basket, 2.25 x 3.75 inches. $80.

Footed milk glass square salt with grape motif. $38.

Squirrel on Nest salt. $25.

Egg Cups

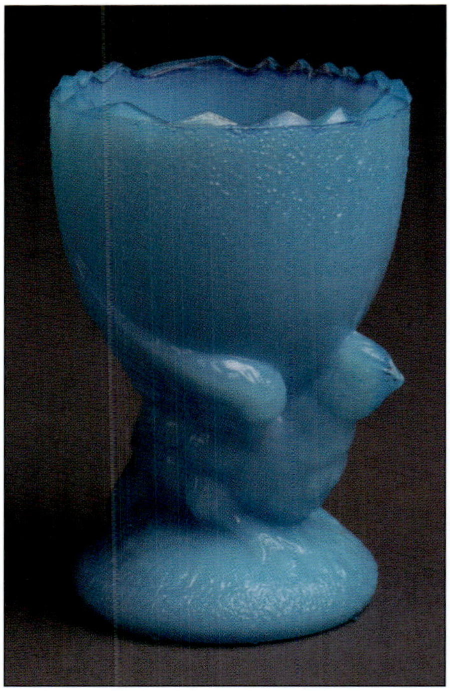

Rare milk glass Chick egg holder. $45.

Blue milk glass egg cup, 3.5 inches. $25.

Egg cup. $38.

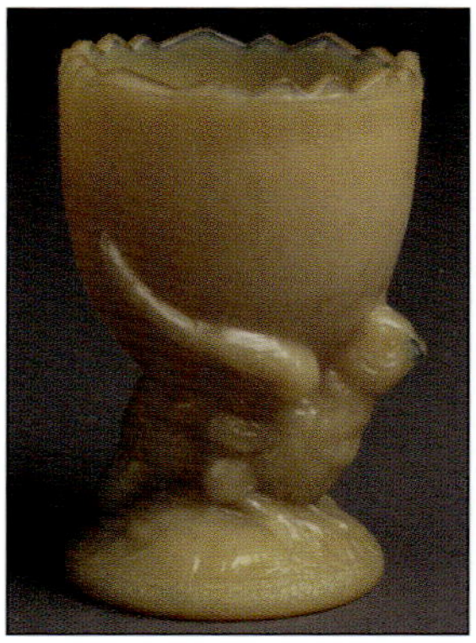

Egg cup. $35.

Toothpicks

Owl with Spread Wings toothpick, 3 inches. $28.

Swan toothpick. $25.

Urn-shaped toothpick in blue milk glass. $28.

Urn-shaped toothpick in slag glass. $28.

Milk glass Handled Basket toothpick holder, 2.5 inches high. $28.

Footed Toothpick in blue milk glass. $28 (new).

Two-inch milk glass Diagonal Bar toothpick holder, 2 inches high. $38.

Footed Tree Stump toothpick. $38.

Black glass toothpick. $35.

Blue milk glass Fiber Bundle toothpick, 2.5 inches. $32.

Horseshoe with Clover toothpick. $38.

Blue milk glass toothpick with foliage. $35.

Two small milk glass covered baskets. $45 each.

Blue milk glass covered vanity jar, 6 inches. $32.

Powder box with brass fitting, 4.5 inches high. $38.

Powder box, 3.5 inches wide. $38.

Powder box, 4.5 inches wide. $42.

Blue powder box, 4.5 inches wide. $42.

Three Kittens, 3 inches square powder box. $125.

Oakleaf powder box with gold paint, 4.5 inches wide. $32.

Lion Head shaving mug with soap cup. $70.

Milk glass Oriental atomizer with metal head. $55.

Shaving Mug. $80.

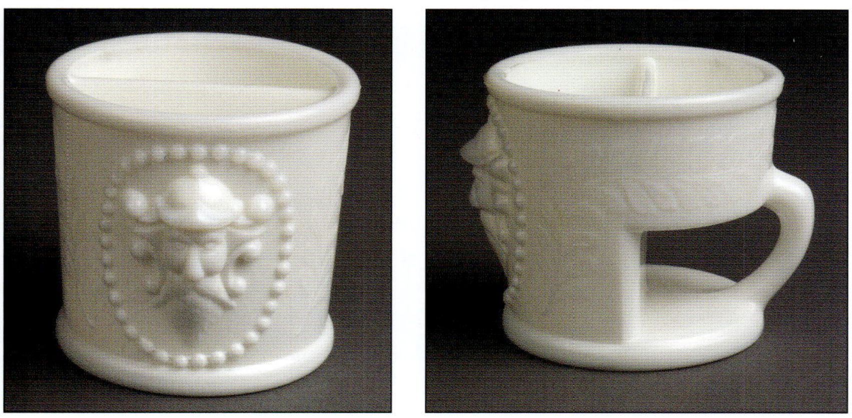

Milk glass Black Face Pomade Jar with feet, top is opaque, bottom is opalescent. $225.

Three piece milk glass Smoking Set, 3.25 x 7.5 inches. $85.

Two milk glass Pipe match holders, 4 inches wide. $45 each.

Blue milk glass Log Cabin match holder with the word "Tecumseh" on one side, 2.5 inches tall. $60.

Milk glass alligator match holder, 3.25 inches wide. $250.

Yellow slag glass match holder (Challinor, Taylor ?). $25.

Carpet Bag wall match holder. $165.

Rose Vase, 5.5 inches high. $35.

Blue milk glass wall pocket. $60.

Blue milk glass Hand vase. $45.

Double Headed Horse vase, 3.75 inches. $42.

Blue milk glass vase, fading paint, 5 inches. $28.

Vase. $38.

French? blue milk glass vase "Tree Trunk with Birds & Berries" embossed, 8.5 inches tall. $60.

Lighting

Milk glass candlestick. $28.

White milk glass finger lamp. $68.

Blue milk glass finger lamp octagonal base. $75.

Blue milk glass finger lamp. $75.

Figural Glass

Blue milk glass easel. $125.

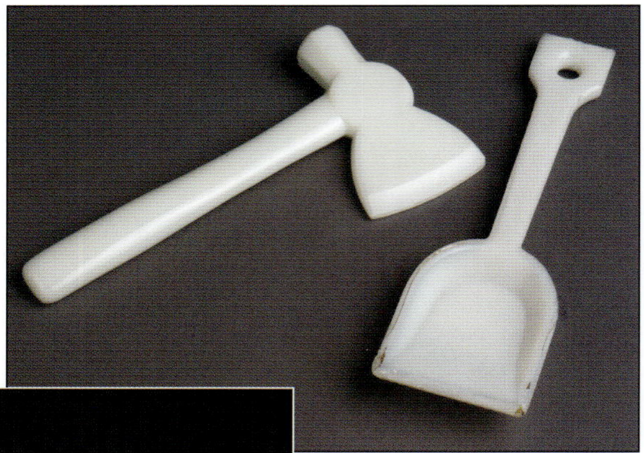

Milk glass pieces spade and hatchet in opal with no paint. $45 each.

Two milk glass Button and Daisy hats, 2.5 inches & 3.5 inches. $28 each.

Milk glass Galloping Horse figurine, circa 1950s. Marked Williams England. $130.

Milk glass Pig paper weight. $55.

Milk glass Pipe "Souvenir of Ravena, N.Y." $42.

Easter Eggs

Glass Easter Egg, large Emerging Chick. $80.

Glass Easter Egg, small, embossed. $80.

Glass Easter Egg, a small Emerging Chick. $80.

Bibliography

Barlow, Raymond E., & Jean E. Kaiser. *The Glass Industry in Sandwich* (Vols. 1-4). Atglen, PA: Schiffer Publishing Ltd., 1983-1989.

Belknap, W.M. *Milk Glass.* New York: Crown Publishers Inc., 1949.

Chiarenza, Frank, & James Slater. *The Milk Glass Book.* Atglen, PA: Schiffer Publishing Ltd., 1998.

Coe, Debbie, & Randy Coe. *Avon's 1876 Cape Cod Collection: Glass Dinnerware.* Atglen, PA: Schiffer Publishing Ltd., 2003.

______. *Glass Animals & Figurines.* Atglen, PA: Schiffer Publishing Ltd., 2003.

Ferson, Regis F., & Mary F. Ferson. Milk Glass Today. Greenburg, PA: Chas. H. Henry Printing Co., 1981.

Garrison, Myrna, & Bob Garrison. *Milk Glass: The Imperial Corporation.* Atglen, PA: Schiffer Publishing Ltd., 2001.

Hardy, Roger, & Claudia Hardy. *The Complete Line of the Akro Agate Co.*

Pickvet, Mark. *The Encyclopedia of Glass.* Atglen, PA: Schiffer Publishing Ltd., 2001.

Piña, Leslie. *Crackle Glass in Color: Depression to '70s.* Atglen, PA: Schiffer Publishing Ltd., 2000.

Sanford, Jo, & Bob Sanford. *Victorian Glass Novelties.* Atglen, PA: Schiffer Publishing Ltd., 2003.

Walk, John. *The Big Book of Fenton Milk Glass, 1940-1985.* Atglen, PA: Schiffer Publishing Ltd., revised edition, 2004.

West Virginia Museum of American Glass, Ltd. *L.G. Wright Glass.* Atglen, PA: Schiffer Publishing Ltd., 2003.